They Welcomed the Child

SERMONS FOR ADVENT AND CHRISTMAS

By

JOHN SCHMIDT

AUGSBURG PUBLISHING HOUSE

Minneapolis, Minnesota

THEY WELCOMED THE CHILD

Scripture quotations are from the Revised Standard Version of the Bible, copyright 1946 and 1952 by the Division of Christian Education of the National Council of Churches.

Hymns from the *Service Book and Hymnal* (SBH) are used by permission of the Commission on the Liturgy and the Hymnal.

Chapter VIII is reprinted by permission from *The Pulpit,* Vol. XXV, No. 12. Copyright 1954 Christian Century Foundation.

MANUFACTURED IN THE UNITED STATES OF AMERICA

CONTENTS

Introduction

A Word of Preparation

"Company's coming!" All of us know what excitement these words bring with them. The guest room is readied. Non-existent or at least invisible dust is wiped off and the carpet dirt is sucked into a vacuum cleaner. Guest linens appear as if by magic. From the oven tantalizing fragrances drift through the entire house.

"Company's coming!" This is the cry of Advent. But do we really need this reminder from the church? Do not the street decorations in every shopping area and the colorful advertisements in our newspapers remind us that "It's only —— days till Christmas"? Do we still need Advent?

The answer must be an emphatic "Yes." For does not the real excitement over coming guests depend, in the last analysis, upon who they are? And does not our welcome of Christmas depend upon whom we expect?

There is a tale of a mother whose little son pestered her for cake. Finally she promised, "You may have as many pieces of cake as you eat slices of bread." With greedy expectation the lad gulped down one slice of bread after another, only to discover, at the last, that he had no appetite left for the cake. This childhood tragedy may be repeated in our experience if we use up so much of our energy and excitement on our preparations for the externals of the holiday that we are too tired to rejoice in the meaning of this great day.

There is danger, obviously, that the purely human joys of the Christmas season will loom so large as to shut all else from our vision. Not that the Christian would—even if he could—ignore this aspect of the Festival. Gifts, family gatherings, loving preparations, and even the brightly decorated Christmas tree are somehow congruous to the great and joyful event this day commemorates. For ought not the whole earth to rejoice when God gives his gift to mankind?

Yet things and our delight in them can cause us to slight the immaterial though eternal treasures that are the abiding meaning of Christmas. We do need to focus our minds, again and again, on the Babe whose coming is the essence of the Christmas fact.

Yet even this may not be enough. It is so easy to become sentimental about a baby. We can coo over it, tickle it under the chin, and feel properly protective for "the dear little, helpless thing." But this misses the point of Christmas, too.

For this day is not an occasion for sentimentality, but for a serious, open-eyed appraisal of ourselves and God. This Child did not remain a helpless baby, dependent on the loving provision and care of his mother. He became a man who "set his face steadfastly" to march to the cross. He rose triumphantly from the tomb, to the unbelief and consternation of disciple and enemy alike. And "he will come again, with glory, to judge both the quick and the dead." No wonder that we must ask ourselves in the words of Paul Gerhardt, "O how shall I receive thee, how greet thee, Lord, aright?"

A glance at the titles which our Advent hymns give our expected Guest would be startling, were we not accustomed to their sound: Emmanuel, Lord of Might, Son of God, lowly King, Judge, King of kings, Savior, Prince of peace, the Lord's Anointed. No ordinary babe, to be sure! This is a king, *the* King whose coming we await.

This is why the message of the church from Advent to the Lord's Epiphany is so awesome. It turns our minds back to the ancient prophecies of which the creeds remind us with the phrase "according to the scriptures." Every longing, every hope, of the heroes of faith, of whom it must still be said, "All these . . . did not receive what was promised, since God had foreseen something better for us" (Hebrews

11:39-40), are brought back to our minds. The promises are indeed fulfilled but even the greatest of their expectations was far less than the fulfillment! "What no eye has seen, nor ear heard, nor the heart of man conceived . . . God has prepared for those who love him" (Isaiah 64:4, 65:17; quoted in 1 Corinthians 2:9). This Jesus, whose birth took place in a crude manger, is truly Lord of all the earth. The manger is the world's most powerful and abiding throne. Almost unnoticed by the power structures of Rome, Athens, or even Jerusalem when he was born —or when he died—Jesus has proved the most durable of his contemporaries. Prelates, procurators, and emperors are remembered because the Nazareth rabbi lived among them.

But even this does not measure the greatness of our Guest. There is another dimension to his coming of which the church must speak.

> *The King shall come when morning dawns*
> *And light triumphant breaks;*
> *When beauty gilds the eastern hills*
> *And life to joy awakes.*
>
> *Not as of old, a little child,*
> *To bear and fight and die;*
> *But crowned with glory like the sun*
> *That lights the morning sky.*
>
> SBH, 10

He is the Triumphant One, whose return in victorious glory we await. This is why the traditional lessons that are read during this season of the year are not concerned with motherhood and birth, with domesticity and "white gifts," but rather with such solemnities as death and judgment, heaven and hell. Drawn not from the infancy narratives but from later pages of the New Testament, they deal with "the last things": the climax of history, the ultimate purposes of God, the eternal victory of the Son. Our Christian expectation is in a cross rather than in a manger, in a risen and reigning Lord rather than in a baby. Unless we see this clearly we cannot understand the nativity as it really is.

The following chapters are intended to reveal this total Christ by encouraging us to see him through the eyes of those who welcomed him—each in his own way—when he first came. This we can do only if we "flesh out" these biblical men and women, giving to them the three-dimensional life they so often lack because of our foolish "reverence" for Bible characters or possibly because of our inability to see them live and talk with the same reality that is ours.

A missionary from northern Rhodesia told of a prayer composed by an African schoolgirl: "O thou Great Chief, light a candle within our hearts that we may see what is therein and sweep the rubbish from thy dwelling place." This is one of the purposes of our observance of Advent and Christmas and we will accomplish it when we see clearly who it is that comes and how decisive our response to him will be.

And there appeared to him an angel of the Lord standing on the right side of the altar of incense. And Zechariah was troubled when he saw him, and fear fell upon him. But the angel said to him, "Do not be afraid, Zechariah, for your prayer is heard, and your wife Elizabeth will bear you a son, and you shall call his name John.

> *And you will have joy and gladness,*
> *and many will rejoice at his birth;*
> *for he will be great before the Lord,*
> *and he shall drink no wine nor strong drink,*
> *and he will be filled with the Holy Spirit,*
> *even from his mother's womb.*
> *And he will turn many of the sons of Israel to the*
> *   Lord their God,*
> *and he will go before him in the spirit and power*
> *   of Elijah,*
> *to turn the hearts of the fathers to the children,*
> *and the disobedient to the wisdom of the just,*
> *to make ready for the Lord a people prepared."*

Luke 1:11-17

Chapter I

The Surprised Priest

Luke 1:5-25, 57-80

The mood of Advent is one of anticipation. We expect a visitor! While there are many who anticipate Christmas with secular interests dominating their thoughts, Christians are reminded by the Advent season of the astonishing gift that makes Christmas a day of great and continuing joy to all the world. Even for Christians this is not easy to keep in mind. "The world is too much with us." Its urgent and skillful appeals crowd upon us through every means of communication. Even the carols that were composed in honor of Christ's birthday are prostituted to swell the profits of merchants. How fitting that the violet paraments in our chancels should remind us of the somber reality of our sin, the sin that makes necessary the coming of Bethlehem's Babe— then and now.

If we are to give him a truly royal welcome, we must look closely at the record of his nativity. There we may see by whom and in what manner he was welcomed at his first advent. And there we may obtain useful hints that will enable us to prepare our hearts and homes for him now.

The first of those whom we meet in the Gospel records is Zechariah. He and his wife Elizabeth were old. Their lives had been full and happy except for the fact that they were childless. The ancient Hebrews regarded this as a mark of divine displeasure, an interpretation which added to their natural sorrow when their union in marriage did not result in children, who would be the incarnation of their oneness. Zechariah and his wife must have puzzled over this fact, for as the Gospel records, "they were both righteous before God, walking in all the commandments and ordinances of the Lord blameless" (Luke 1:6).

I

This is the man whom we see first in the silence of doubt.

It all began in the temple at Jerusalem. Zechariah was a priest, a member of the family that held this hereditary office. The number of these descendants of Aaron was then about twenty thousand, so their service in the temple was only occasional. It should be remembered that only in this temple were priestly services required. The synagogues that had sprung up in every community since the Exile served a very different purpose. They existed for religious education, not for sacrifices, and they were served by rabbis.

It was therefore a great day when Zechariah received word that he would have the opportunity to serve in his priestly capacity. His particular appointment was determined by lot. His was to place a sacrifice upon the altar of incense. Even though this was done every morning and evening, before the sacrifice of a lamb, it was for him a once-in-a-lifetime opportunity. This responsibility he carried out and in connection with it spoke the prescribed liturgical prayers. It seems likely that the angel's words, "Your prayer is heard," imply that after this public responsibility had been fulfilled, Zechariah took advantage of his presence in the holy place to pray once again that a son might be given them. It was a prayer that no doubt had come often from his lips. And, possibly, his added petition concerned also the speedy coming of God's Messiah, for whom Israel had waited so long.

While we cannot be certain about the content of Zechariah's prayer, we can be sure he did not expect his prayer to be answered! His astonishment and fear are evidence of that. But before we scorn him for his weak faith, let us look quickly at ourselves. How many worshipers bring their umbrellas along when they come to church to pray for a rain to end a long drought? Or why, after you have prayed God "to send forth laborers into his harvest," are you shocked when your own son or daughter decides to prepare for full-time service in the church? Have you muttered, "The church is always asking for money," when increased budgets are needed to carry on the enlarged program which God has given your church in answer to your prayers? Do you not expect God to take your prayers seriously and answer them? In this respect, most of us fall under the same judgment as does Zechariah. The reproach of Jesus applies to us all: "O man of little faith, why did you doubt?" (Matt. 14:31).

There is some excuse for Zechariah, of course. He was a victim of the paralysis of long delay. As far as his personal hopes were concerned, the prayer for a son was largely a matter of habit. If his union with Elizabeth had been barren during their youthful years, how could he expect any change when they were old? As to the promised Messiah, no doubt he would come some day, but why assume that he would come just now? So many pious generations had prayed and hoped and waited in vain. The mood of Zechariah and most of his contemporaries toward Christ's first advent is almost identical with ours toward his second advent. We do not doubt it, but we do not really expect it, either. Our attitude—and theirs—is perfectly pictured in the words of 2 Peter: "Where is the promise of his coming? For ever since the fathers fell asleep, all things have continued as they were from the beginning of creation" (3:4). Nothing had happened for so long that Zechariah

had unconsciously concluded that nothing ever would happen.

But it did. The angel who appeared at the right side of the altar of incense came with a magnificent promise. It welded into one the separate yearnings of this aged priest. He would have a son and this son was to become the special messenger of God. He would proclaim the immediate coming of the Messiah. Through his preaching he would "make ready for the Lord a people prepared" (Luke 1:17). A son for himself and the Messiah for his people—what an answer to prayer this was!

It was too good to believe, and Zechariah did not believe it. Quite bluntly and realistically he told Gabriel, "I am an old man and my wife is advanced in years" (v. 18). The objection sounded so reasonable and final—if one leaves God out.

But God will not be left out. Since Zechariah insisted on proof, he was given unwelcome evidence that God meant what he said. "You will be silent and unable to speak until the day that these things come to pass, because you did not believe my words, which will be fulfilled in their time" (v. 20). Thus the silence of doubt fell upon the priest.

When he came out of the sanctuary, he could not give the customary blessing to the worshipers who stood waiting. They were dismissed with a gesture. Soon after Zechariah's period of service had been completed, the child was conceived, but the gift of speech was not restored to the father until after the child's birth. It was a joyful time. There was rejoicing among friends and relatives "that the Lord had shown great mercy to her [Elizabeth], and they rejoiced with her" (v. 58).

A week later the ceremony of circumcision was held and the question of the child's name arose. "Zechariah, like his father," they suggested. But Elizabeth, to whom her husband had of course told every detail of the angel's message through written notes, insisted that he must be called John. Forgetting in their excitement that the father's hearing had not been affected and remembering only that the dumb usually suffer also from deafness, "they made signs to his father, inquiring what he would have him called." His answer, written on a tablet, was emphatic, "His name is John" (vv. 62-63).

II

At that moment the silence of doubt gave way to the speech of faith.

The emotions that had of necessity been bottled up within Zechariah for months, now found their first adequate expression. The words of the Benedictus (vv. 68-79) reflect both his fervent meditation upon what had been told him by Gabriel and his familiarity with the poetic and prophetic literature of the Old Testament. As a result, his exalted thoughts found fitting verbal garments.

"Blessed be the Lord God of Israel, for he has visited and redeemed his people," he begins. His joy that at last his son is born is absorbed in the greater joy that God has now carried out the great promises that "he spoke by the mouth of his holy prophets from of old." No trace remains of the doubt that had made even his prayers into an empty formality. Gone was the dullness that had covered his own expectations, and had made him one with his faithless contemporaries. The promised King was at hand. In a sense that no earlier prophet or ruler had been, he would be *the* Anointed of God, designated by him to accomplish his will among men. This is the meaning both of the Hebrew "Messiah" and the Greek "Christ" which the Bible and the church have ascribed to Jesus of Nazareth.

He would be greater than David. We need not wonder that Zechariah shared, at least partially, the presuppositions of his day, that this Messiah would be the strong conqueror of Israel's enemies. ". . . that we should be saved from our enemies, and from the hand of all who hate us." No people as ardently patriotic as the Jews and living under the oppressive hand of an alien conqueror, could fail to place that interpretation on the ancient promises. The records of our Lord's ministry show clearly how difficult this idea was to uproot. Jesus' refusal to conform to the desired pattern constituted the major obstacle to his "success."

With much less excuse, we moderns also find it

difficult to accept the truth that our real and most dangerous enemies are not material but spiritual. Also, we are usually much more concerned about the needs and desires of our bodies than of our souls. The way we spend our money proves it. "Things temporal" seem so much more real than "things spiritual." It should, therefore, be easy for us to understand Zechariah.

Yet he was wrong in his expectation. As our Lord himself insisted, "My kingship is not of this world" (John 18:36). He is not a competitor, *at their level,* with the Pilates, the Neros or the Stalins of the world, even though his lordship inevitably challenges the evil in their systems. He, like his followers, contends not "against flesh and blood, but against the principalities, against the powers, against the world rulers of this present darkness, against the spiritual hosts of wickedness in the heavenly places" (Eph. 6:12).

In all fairness, it must be said that there is a hint of this in Zechariah's Benedictus: ". . . to grant us that we, being delivered from the hand of our enemies, might serve him without fear, in holiness and righteousness before him all the days of our life." Little wonder that his heart overflowed with joyful gratitude at the prospect of such a gift!

His mood of exultation recedes for a moment as he looks lovingly into the face of his son, whom he has now perhaps taken into his arms: "And you,

child, will be called the prophet of the Most High."
What an honor to his house! There had been no
prophetic voice in Israel in four centuries. Now God
had sent another—his son.

Yes, miracle piled upon miracle. For, as though the
dignity of the prophetic office were not enough, his
son was to have a solitary and supreme place among
the prophets of God. His specific assignment was to
prepare the way for the King. As court officials
preceded their ruler on a journey to make certain
that his road was both safe and comfortable, John
was to serve the Christ. Other prophets had only
been able to say, "He will come," but John's words
would be, "He is here!" So Zechariah continues,
"You will go before the Lord to prepare his ways, to
give knowledge of salvation to his people in the
forgiveness of their sins, through the tender mercy
of our God."

Some prophets had been given somber messages
of judgment. It is even true that a few seem to have
found this message to their taste. Certainly Jonah
did not desire any moderation of his outcry, "Yet
forty days, and Nineveh shall be overthrown!" (Jonah
3:4). He objected only that warning should be given
to these heathen and that God should prove merciful
when they repented. Nor is it easy to detect much
reluctance in Amos' prophecy of the impending
doom of the Northern Kingdom. But there were
others whose hearts wept at the harsh message that

they were called upon to deliver. Hosea and Jeremiah did not consider the possibility of softening the word they were given to preach, any more than a telegraph operator presumes to change the wording of a telegram that begins, "The Secretary of the Army has asked me to express his deep regret . . ." because he knows the message will bring sadness into a home. God's message was inviolate. Yet these men were in tears when they preached their message of certain judgment upon a nation they loved.

How different from their message was the commission of Zechariah's son! His was to be the initial proclamation of that "good news of a great joy which shall come to all the people" (Luke 2:10) through the birth of the Savior. John was to be the first in the long line of preachers of the Gospel of God's amazing grace. He could announce the astounding fact that God's holiness had bowed down to lift up sinful man. He could point to the "Lamb of God," the first and the only effective sacrifice for the sin of the world. He was to preach that truth which "angels vainly seek to comprehend."

Little wonder that Zechariah compares the coming of this glorious, new fact with the dawning of a new day. "The day shall dawn upon us from on high to give light to those who sit in darkness and in the shadow of death, to guide our feet into the way of peace." The Light of the world has come! No wonder the silence of doubt is now done away with and the speech of faith has taken its place.

On Jordan's banks the Baptist's cry
Announces that the Lord is nigh;
Awake and hearken, for he brings
Glad tidings of the King of kings.

Then cleansed be every breast from sin,
Make straight the way for God within;
And let us all our hearts prepare
For Christ to come and enter there.

SBH, 4

But when he saw many of the Pharisees and Sadducees coming for baptism, he said to them, "You brood of vipers! Who warned you to flee from the wrath to come? Bear fruit that befits repentance, and do not presume to say to yourselves, 'We have Abraham as our father'; for I tell you, God is able from these stones to raise up children to Abraham. Even now the ax is laid to the root of the trees; every tree therefore that does not bear good fruit is cut down and thrown into the fire.

"I baptize you with water for repentance, but he who is coming after me is mightier than I, whose sandals I am not worthy to carry; he will baptize you with the Holy Spirit and with fire. His winnowing fork is in his hand, and he will clear his threshing floor and gather his wheat into the granary, but the chaff he will burn with unquenchable fire."

Matt. 3:7-12

Chapter II

The Wilderness Voice

Matthew 3:1-12

Preaching can be dull. When that is true, it is, normally, the preacher who is dull. This is wholly forgotten by the man who apologizes in advance, "I'm not going to preach." Why shouldn't he preach? Preaching ought to be exciting. The ministry of John the Baptist offers proof that it can be.

This prophet of the advent is a startling and a unique figure. Can you think of another successful preacher who got as far away from his congregation as possible, only to have it follow him far into the country? Or one who called his socially prominent hearers a "brood of vipers"? Had he never learned how to make friends and influence people? Or might it be true, as George Buttrick once said, that people are not driven from the church by stern truths that make them uneasy but rather by weak nothings that make them contemptuous?* John's career would support such a view.

I

The Baptist's preaching had but two themes. The first of these was a call to repentance.

The Jews of the first century heard a great deal of preaching. Theirs was the first religious cult in the Mediterranean world of which that could be said. All others, including Hebrew religion before the Babylonian Exile, had no preaching. In the non-Jewish religions, the cultic life centered in a temple that was considered the residence of the deity. Here his statue normally stood, and here sacrifices were offered. There were no congregations of worshipers, but only individuals who came to sacrifice or pray. This was true also of Hebrew religion before the Exile, except that only "heretics" like Aaron and Jeroboam dared to put a statue of God in the inner sanctuary. Out of the experience of the Exile had come something new and valuable. Synagogues were established in every community where Jews could gather to hear their Scriptures explained and applied by competent teachers.

The contemporaries of John had therefore heard many sermons, but none like this. John's preaching was not a tiresome repetition of well-worn platitudes or the mumbling of traditional formulas. It did not consist of quotations from this authority and that; neither did it lose itself in dialectical hair-splitting. John had something definite to say, a message that had been committed to him by God. In direct, unvarnished words he speaks to his hearers. They could not take refuge in any vague, poetical phrasing, but could only acknowledge, "There was a man sent from God whose name was John" (John 1:6).

His preaching was as inescapable—and possibly as irritating—as an alarm clock. Finding his people in the sleep of self-congratulation, he cried out, "Wake, awake, for night is flying!" He would have understood the warning issued by the Lutheran bishops of Norway during the Nazi occupation of that land when they said: "Harmlessly edifying preaching would be a denial of God." The fact that he knew that real preaching might be dangerous did not deter him.

His words flash like lightning, as he warns vigorously of "the wrath to come." Already the gardener has his ax blade at the trunk of every unfruitful tree. Within moments it will be cut down and burned because it failed in the purpose for which it was planted. The thresher is already at work with his winnowing fork, throwing the grain high into the air so that the chaff will be blown away and the wheat itself will fall to the threshing floor. No one could fall asleep during such sermons, nor could conscience fall asleep.

John's sermons could surely be described, as were those of Puritan preachers in Britain's "Golden Age," as "painful." The contrast was marked between this Puritan preaching and that of the established church. As Anthony Gilbert's parson puts it, "As for my Lord (his noble patron) I heard him say that he could

never go to any of these Geneva sermons that he
came quiet home, but that there was ever something that pricked his conscience; he always thought
that they made their whole sermon against him. But
in the reading of Matins and Evensong at St. Paul's
or in my reading of my service in his chapel, he
sayeth, he feeleth no such thing, for he is never
touched, but goeth merrily to his dinner." But isn't
it the responsibility of a Christian sermon, "to afflict
the comfortable" as well as "to comfort the afflicted"?
John seems to have thought so.

He indulged in no empty generalities that offer
such large loopholes that hearers could easily escape.
Even the brief reports given us in the New Testament indicate how directly he applied his message
to different groups of listeners. He isolated tax-collectors, soldiers, Pharisees, and Sadducees and spoke
to the specific temptations and needs of each. He
fitted the shoes carefully to each customer. He knew
that a religious discourse does not become a true
sermon until it points its "You are the man" (2 Sam.
12:7) at each hearer. It is here that so much modern
preaching fails. It is content to give information, true
and needful perhaps, but still impersonal and ab-
stract. It is, as someone has expressed it, "preaching
in the third person." John's never was. He talked to
men, and they knew it.

Yet, in so doing, he treated everyone alike. He
knew that "God shows no partiality" (Rom. 2:11)
and, like the one who had sent him, he was unim-

pressed by human measures of attainment and fame. The sharp words that Matthew reports as being spoken to the Pharisees and Sadducees are related also by Luke, who says that John was "accustomed to say" these things to "the multitude." Every preacher knows the easy temptation to denounce vigorously the sins of distant people. It is much safer and more popular to condemn "secularistic and materialistic Communism," for example, than to point to the secularism and materialism of our own capitalistic culture. Preaching at absentees serves to give a congregation the comfortable feeling of self-righteousness. But is it the task of the Christian pulpit to create more Pharisees?

John's audiences, like every similar assembly, sought for refuge from his blasting words. But John demolished these bomb-shelters one by one. A favorite of the Hebrews had always been the fact that they were descendants of Abraham. Were they not therefore entitled to share in all the glorious promises made to him? This was a security no one could take away. A common boast was: "A single Israelite is of more worth in God's sight than all the nations of the world." Looking for an apt illustration, John sees the abundant supply of loose stones that lay everywhere in the Jordan wilderness. "Children of Abraham? Rather, as your conduct shows, children of snakes! Don't you know that God is able to transform these stones into children of Abraham?" It should be noted in passing, so that we do not sidestep the vigor of John's message by attributing it to mere verbal extravagance, that Jesus Christ himself used identical language against the same antagonists (Matt. 12:34; 23:33).

The very baptism upon which this wilderness preacher insisted had this significance. Baptism was known to the Jews of that day. In fact, it was one of three requirements made of Gentiles who became converts to Judaism, the other two being circumcision and the offering of sacrifice. The Dead Sea scrolls reveal the existence of a cultic retreat where a form af daily baptism was observed. But what John was saying was that not only "unclean" Gentiles but also "clean" Jews were in need of this washing of repentance. "For there is no distinction; since all have sinned and fall short of the glory of God . . ." (Rom. 3:21, 22). How shocking—no difference between Jew and Gentile, between Russian and American, between capitalist and beggar, between Negro and Caucasian? "None," says John's voice, firmly. There are no family trees high enough, no iron curtains solid enough to keep out this word of divine judgment.

There is still another notable feature of the preaching of this wilderness prophet. He expects results. Of course, every preacher should, for he goes out in the name of one who said, "My word . . . shall not return to me empty, but it shall accomplish that which I purpose, and prosper in the thing for which I sent it" (Isa. 55:11). Yet there are so many of us, in the pulpit as well as in the pew, who have no sense of expectancy when a sermon is preached. We expect nothing to happen and, naturally, nothing does.

Someone has given a cruel definition of music as "an art that moves one greatly to nothing in particular." That does, indeed, seem to be the curse of most of the arts. We see a "realistic" movie, for example, that makes vivid one of the areas of great need or clarifies a recurring human tragedy. We "enjoy a good cry" over it, but that is all. Nothing happens; nothing is expected to happen. The only reason the film was made was to induce you to buy an admission ticket, and you have already done that.

Preaching is much more than an art. It is a technique for getting things done. John's preaching was intended to bring men to repentance. That goes much deeper than tears of sorrow. Repentance, in the New Testament, means to change one's mind, to face about, to move in the opposite direction.

The Advent prophet made that very clear. "Bear fruit that befits repentance" (Matt. 3:8). God's will is not withdrawal from life, but helpful participation in it. The luxury of a second tunic is sinful if there are those who have none. Food, likewise, is to be shared with the needy. John did not shrink from nailing down these truths in terms of the occupational temptations of his hearers. Tax-collectors, who had a well-earned reputation as grafters, were told to be honest. They should collect only such taxes as the law provided. Soldiers were told that they must not rob others by threat of violence or by blackmail. They must be content with their official wages. And since he did not hesitate to proclaim the truth to the powerful, he said to King Herod, who was infatuated with Herodias, the wife of his brother Philip, "It is not lawful for you to have her" (Matt. 14:4).

The contemporary preacher has much to learn from the preaching of John the Baptist. In a day when the holy requirements of the Holy One are denied by many and ignored by even more, the message of judgment and repentance is certainly required. No preacher of the truth of God can stand silent before brazen evil, whether individual or corporate. The eternal demand of God is: "You shall be holy, for I am holy" (1 Peter 1:16).

A message of judgment is incomplete, surely, but in such a world as this it must be heard.

II

The second theme of these first Advent sermons is specifically Christian: The King is here!

This, in fact, was the very basis for the ministry of John. As his father Zechariah had said, he was sent to make the highway of the coming King level, straight, and smooth. This activity had been forecast by an earlier prophet: "The voice of one crying in the wilderness: Prepare the way of the Lord, make his paths straight. Every valley shall be filled, and every mountain and hill shall be brought low, and the crooked shall be made straight, and the rough ways shall be made smooth; and all flesh shall see the salvation of God" (Luke 3:4-6, cited from Isa. 40:3-5). It is this that explains his sharp words of judgment. Israel's Messiah was no silly Russian Empress to be deceived on her journey by false facades and by serfs dressed in unaccustomed finery and forced to smile by the threatening whips of imperial troops. He seeks reality. There must be genuine repentance, a real turning from sin to God.

All the Gospels indicate the marked contrast between the fearless bearing of John before others and his humility before the Christ. "He who is mightier than I is coming, the thong of whose sandals I am not worthy to untie," he said (Luke 3:16). When Jesus sought him out and desired baptism at his hands, this fiery prophet protested, "I need to be baptized by you, and do you come to me?" (Matt. 3:14). Later, when he was subjected to the hardest test that can come to a man who has known popular success, he could still say, "He who has the bride is the bridegroom; the friend of the bridegroom, who stands and hears him, rejoices greatly at the bridegroom's voice; therefore this joy of mine is now full. He must increase, but I must decrease" (John 3:29-30). At a human level, this is perhaps the supreme test of greatness—and John passes it with flying colors!

Emphatically he rejected the suggestion that he might himself be the expected Messiah, even when the question was put to him officially by a deputation of priests and Levites from Jerusalem (John 1:19-28). No, the true Messiah, whose coming he announced, would divide humanity as a thresher separates grain from chaff. With a winnowing fork the beaten grain will be thrown high so that the wind will blow the chaff and straw to one side, where it can be destroyed by fire.

Even the baptism of the Christ would be different and greater than that of his prophet. John's baptism was like that of the Jordan water that he used—cold and incapable of giving life. It was symbolic of cleansing, but could not really make man clean of sin. That could be done only by Christian baptism, "with the Holy Spirit and with fire" (Luke 3:16). "Fire" is an appropriate symbol, of course, because it purifies precious metal from the alloy with which it is combined and destroys the unworthy. This, said John, would be the result of the coming of the expected Christ.

We cannot overlook the fact that John did not fully understand him whose advent he proclaimed. That became clear later when he lay in prison, awaiting the death that the embittered Herodias had plotted. Like many others he took offense at the simplicity and humility of Jesus. Instead of the all-dominating ruler he had expected, he saw one who "wasted" his time teaching and healing peasants and who was either unable or unwilling to protect himself against the scheming hatred of the powerful. So weak was he, or so lacking in gratitude, that he even permitted his herald to lie in a dirty prison. So John asked, "Are you he who is to come, or shall we look for another?" (Matt. 11:3).

This is part of the "scandal" of the Gospel. It has always been "a stumbling-block to Jews and folly to Gentiles" (1 Cor. 1:23). Jesus makes no attempt to evade the issue, for he tells John's disciples to return to their master and tell him that they had seen precisely those things that had caused questions to arise. "And blessed is he who takes no offense at me." John's doubt does not mean that Jesus must change his program. It means, rather, that John must have his mind changed concerning the true nature of Christ's mission. He must return to an earlier insight and think through its implications.

The Baptist had seen, so John the Evangelist tells us, that this mighty King was to sacrifice himself. "Behold the Lamb of God, who takes away the sin of the world!" (1:29). He would be both priest and sacrifice. The thousands of spotless lambs, brought to the great altar of sacrifice in Jerusalem by pilgrims who sought release from their burden of guilt were a silent prophecy of the effective and final sacrifice whose blood would atone for the sin of all men.

Here is the true climax of the ministry of the Advent prophet. This is the real and abiding greatness of his preaching. It does not lie in the size of the congregations who gathered in the wilderness, nor in the number of those who submitted to his baptism. Rather, it becomes clear in the outstretched fore-finger and the awed tones that directed his disciples to Jesus, "Behold, the Lamb of God!" For he is the goal and fulfillment of all prophecy, including John's.

For the herald's voice is crying
  In the desert far and near,
Bidding all men to repentance,
  Since the kingdom now is here.
Oh, that warning cry obey!
  Now prepare for God a way!
Let the valleys rise to meet him,
  And the hills bow down to greet him.

Make ye straight what long was crooked,
  Make the rougher places plain;
Let your hearts be true and humble,
  As befits his holy reign. . . .

SBH, 12

---

*George A. Buttrick, *Jesus Came Preaching*. Charles Scribner's Sons, New York, N.Y.

And he came to her and said, "Hail, O favored one, the Lord is with you!" But she was greatly troubled at the saying, and considered in her mind what sort of greeting this might be. And the angel said to her, "Do not be afraid, Mary, for you have found favor with God. . . ." And Mary said,

"My soul magnifies the Lord,
and my spirit rejoices in God my Savior,
for he has regarded the low estate of his handmaiden.
For behold, henceforth all generations will call me
    blessed;
for he who is mighty has done great things for me,
and holy is his name."

Luke 1:28-30, 46-49

Chapter III

The Virgin Mother

Luke 1:26-38, 46-55

There has been a virtual conspiracy of silence within Protestant churches regarding the virgin mother of our Lord. Of course, this silence is a reaction against the false and excessive veneration paid to her by the Church of Rome. But the sad result is still that the woman whom God selected to be the mother of the Savior should be sinned against doubly—by one group which honors her far above her merits and by another which, in effect, declines to honor her at all. May we not, in this Advent season, thinking of those who welcomed our Lord at his first coming, pay her the balanced and true honor that the Scriptures do?

I

The Bible speaks, first, as we must, of the greatness of Mary.

We should make it clear that Mary's real greatness lies in the splendor of the gift given to her.

When the angel Gabriel came to announce the miraculous conception of her Son, he addressed her as the "favored one." Yet the weight and emphasis of his message is on her Son, who "will be great, and will be called the Son of the Most High" (Luke 1:32). Mary's own words in the Magnificat show how conscious she was of her nothingness in the presence of God. As Luther comments, she magnifies God, but minimizes herself. She felt favored indeed, because *God* had come to her; she felt humbled because God had come to *her*. "He has . . . exalted those of low degree; he has filled the hungry with good things" (vv. 52-53).

When the early church decided at Chalcedon that the Virgin Mary might rightly be called "the mother of God," the intention was not to assert the glory of Mary. Rather, it was the glory of her Son that was being asserted and defended. It was the council's way of asserting boldly that in the Babe of Bethlehem "the whole fulness of deity dwells bodily" (Col. 2:9), that he is "God of God, Light of Light, very God of very God." It is in this sense also that the Lutheran confessions approve this historic phrase. He to whom Mary gave birth is "true God, Son of the Father from eternity," as Luther's Small Catechism confesses, so that Mary may properly be called "the mother of God." Only a perverted use of this ancient expression has caused Protestants to look upon it with reserve. Mary is "the mother of

God," not because she was great, but because God is gracious.

The words "Blessed are you among women" (Luke 1:42) do not suggest that Mary was free from sin (immaculately conceived), for the identical phrase is used of Jael who hammered a nail into the temple of Sisera (Judges 5:24). Must this bloody-handed patriot also be considered free from sinful origin and action?

Having thus put the emphasis where Scripture places it, we may safely add that God was not careless in selecting an earthly mother for his Son. Mary was a young woman of simple piety and trust. The source of this faith can be seen in the Magnificat, in which we discern how the mind of this maiden was saturated in the Psalter and the Prophets. Her joyful exclamation of thanksgiving, praise, and astonishment finds natural and fitting expression in the words of ancient Scripture.

It is apparent that the announcement of the angel startled her. The biological miracle was as bewildering to her as to any modern critic—"How can this be, since I have no husband?" Yet, believing with all her heart that with God nothing will be impossible, Mary bows to the divine will with the simple words, "Behold, I am the handmaid of the Lord; let it be to me according to your word" (vv. 34, 38).

A young woman who had grown up, as Mary had, in a small peasant village would have no illusions concerning the consequences of this decision. There must have been in her mind, in the first place, a very realistic uncertainty as to Joseph's response to this situation. They loved one another and had already pledged each other their troth in a formal engagement. But what would happen now? Would he believe her story of the angel and his amazing message? Or would he assume, as indeed he had every right to do, that she was telling this fantastic tale to avoid confessing her sexual misconduct with another? Joseph was "a just man" (Matt. 1:19) who honored and obeyed the Law, and that Law imposed a death penalty upon one who was convicted of violating the bond of marriage. Would Joseph's love and understanding be sufficient for such a test? Mary could not answer these questions, no matter how urgently they forced themselves upon her. Joseph's response was cloaked in uncertainty.

There was, however, no uncertainty about the response of her fellow villagers. Most of them would leap upon her as ruthlessly as wolves fall upon a wounded companion. Driven by self-righteousness or by perverted anger toward one who dared to carry out their own unexpressed desires, they would make her life miserable during the coming months. They would, in all likelihood, pour out their bitterness even upon her Child. She had heard cruel expressions directed at other unfortunate children and she might well shrink at the thought of their being spoken to one of her own flesh and blood.

Yet in obedient and simple piety she assumed the "cross" that is always present for the true disciple. If God's will for her led through this scandal and his purposes could be attained in this way only, she must reply, "Thy will, not mine, be done." Her Son may well have been thinking of his mother's experience when he taught, "Blessed are you when men . . . utter all kinds of evil against you falsely on my account. Rejoice and be glad, for your reward is great in heaven" (Matt. 5:11, 12).

Mary was great because she willingly surrendered her body to God for his use. But as Luther said, she was great also because she was "pregnant in soul." The whole of her life was glorified and enriched by God's coming into it. There has always been an unbiblical piety that finds "spirituality" only in the denial and suppression of ordinary and natural living. Such piety requires that the virgin mother be "lifted above" the normal conditions of life. Therefore a natural marital relation between Mary and her husband had to be denied and an explanation manufactured to "explain" the other children in their home. Eventually this demand culminated in the unscriptural claims that Mary was herself conceived without taint of original sin and that her body, after death, did not decay in a grave but was "assumed" into heaven. It is significant that the papal proclamations of these dogmas made no effort to sustain these claims by biblical evidence. Instead they depended on the top-heavy logic that says: "God could have done this; it is fitting that he should have done this; therefore he did do it."

Of all this the Scriptures and evangelical Christianity know nothing. Rather, the greatness of the Virgin is to be seen in the simplicity of her life. She is not truly honored by being described in pious legend as the "perpetual virgin," but rather when she is seen performing the simple yet vital tasks that fell to the wife of a village carpenter and the mother of a growing family of sons and daughters. In Luther's vivid words, "She did her work as usual, milked the cows, cooked, washed dishes and swept the floor." For the Bible and the Reformers know that the family, with its natural functions and privileges, is established by God to be the arena within which men and women are to serve one another and so to serve him. The truly devout life does not consist in a flight from ordinary life, but in a willing acceptance of its possibilities and its limitations. Mary's greatness, then, is derived in part from her faithful acceptance of God's will for her and from her affirmation of family life.

Yet it must be added, in the words of Augustine, that "Mary was more blessed in that she believed in Christ, than in that she had given him birth." She herself found that fact hard to remember. But Augustine's words rest upon the direct statement of her Son: "My mother and my brothers are those who hear the word of God and do it" (Luke 8:21). Mary is a saint only because she believes in her Son and received eternal life from his hand. Were it not for this, it would have to be said of her what Jesus said of John the Baptist: "He who is least in the kingdom of God is greater than he" (Luke 7:28).

II

Just as clearly as the Bible speaks of Mary's greatness, it points to the limitations of the virgin mother.

Mary could not always live at the peak of her religion. There were moments when the unbounded humility of the Magnificat was forgotten. Mary herself forgets "the low estate of [God's] handmaiden" and comes to presume upon the unique privilege that had been granted her. Like us, she falls into the temptation of acting as though God's goodness comes because of our human deserving, rather than from his undeserved grace.

How natural, then, that she should presume upon her relation at the Cana wedding feast—and how wrong. It seemed such a simple thing to suggest that her Son use his power to solve the problem of their hosts. It was really a compliment that she should be sure that he was able to deal with such a situation. "They have no wine." Yet how sharp the rebuke contained in Jesus' reply, "O woman, what have you to do with me? My hour has not yet come" (John 2:3-4). His mother, yes, but she must not forget for a moment that he is nevertheless her Lord. She had forgotten that God is not a respecter of per-

sons and that what he has done for her he will do
for all mankind. It is true that God "has regarded
the low estate of his handmaiden," but that fact may
not be separated from the adjoining statement that
"his mercy is on those who fear him from generation
to generation" (Luke 1:48, 50).

Most scholars are convinced from a study of three
parallel accounts of the later ministry of Jesus (Matt.
12:46-50, Mark 3:31-35, Luke 8:19-21) that at a
critical moment, when even Jesus' friends were saying, "He is beside himself" and his enemies cried,
"He has an unclean spirit," his own family lost faith
in Jesus and intended to persuade him to give up a
ministry that aroused such opposition. That would
explain why Jesus, with surprising lack of courtesy,
refused to go out to them and turned instead to his
disciples with the words, "Here are my mother and
my brothers! Whoever does the will of God is my
brother, and sister, and mother" (Mark 3:34, 35).

But is it conceivable that Mary, after the experience of the angelic annunciation, should have yield-
ed to unbelief? How could she forget the glorious
words, "He will be great, and will be called the
Son of the Most High; and the Lord God will give
to him the throne of his father David, and he will
reign over the house of Jacob for ever; and of his
kingdom there will be no end" (Luke 1:32-33)? We
must not forget the fact that these words were
dulled by the passage of thirty years, during which
time Jesus "was obedient to" his parents (2:51),

living a completely normal life within the family and community. We may recall also that John the Baptist had similar difficulty in reconciling what he saw of the humble and disregarded Jesus with the high expectations he had held of Israel's King and Christ. Possibly Mary's difficulty came from the same source.

Mary, like every other human being except her Son, is a sinner. Like us, she needs grace. Certainly she cannot bestow it on others. Nothing in Scripture justifies, even slightly, the extravagant claims made for her by the Roman Church. Cardinal Stritch of Chicago approved with his *imprimatur* a "Novena in Honor of the Immaculate Heart of our Lady of Fatima" that reads, in part, "Thou art the Gate of Heaven, O Mother beloved; no one shall enter save through thee." A booklet describing the virtues of a medal of the Virgin, approved by Cardinal Daugherty, reads, "The dying clasp it to their hearts with the assurance that Mary, Gate of Heaven, will lead them to eternal bliss." One of Rome's most honored teachers, St. Alphonsus Liguori, spoke of her as the one "at whose command all things obey, even God." Can greater blasphemy put on the garments of piety?

A wooing voice of Rome closed a broadcast with these words, "On the last day, when we go before God for judgment, we shall hear him say the most consoling words of all, and the pledge of our eternal salvation, 'I've heard my Mother speak of you.'"

But the Lord Jesus does not share his grace and power with any other. "There is one God, and there is one mediator between God and men, the man Christ Jesus, who gave himself as a ransom for all" (1 Tim. 2:5). Against such false teaching we must bear our evangelical witness today as emphatically as did Luther four centuries ago. Unfortunately, Rome has not changed, except to have taken increasing strides toward becoming a cult of Mary, rather than a Christian church. Certain bishops and theologians at Vatican II sought to stem this popular movement, yet several American prelates have chosen as the motto on their coats of arms the words "Per Maria ad Christum" ("through Mary to Christ").

Against every such attempt to subtract from the unique splendor of the grace and power of the Lord Jesus Christ we must protest. We must assert with full assurance and profound emphasis the words our Lord really spoke, that contrast so markedly with those attributed to him by Rome's spokesman: "Truly, truly, I say to you, I am the door to the sheep. . . . if any one enters by me, he will be saved, and will go in and out and find pasture. . . . I am the way, and the truth, and the life; no one comes to the Father, but by me" (John 10:7, 9; 14:6). We do not honor Mary by denying her Son, but rather by heeding her words, "Do whatever he tells you" (John 2:5).

Rabbinical tradition tells us that out of profound reverence the ancient Hebrews decorated with gold and gems the flute on which Moses played during his shepherd days. But this encrustation closed all the apertures, so that no music ever again came from it. That is true, likewise, of the legendary honors that have been heaped upon Mary in some sections of the church. The village housewife of Nazareth knew nothing, and would have wanted to know nothing, of such dignities. She is no "Queen of Heaven," like the pagan goddesses Isis and Astarte, but a child of God, through the merciful grace of her Son. We dare not repeat the false Ave Maria that the church composed in the sixteenth century and which assumes that she is in a singular position to pray to (or to command) her Son. Rather, we repeat, gratefully, the *biblical* Ave Maria: "Hail, O favored one, the Lord is with you!" (Luke 1:28).

We honor her most truly when we repeat her words: "My soul magnifies the Lord, and my spirit rejoices in God my Savior, for he has regarded the low estate of his handmaiden. For behold, henceforth all generations will call me blessed; for he who is mighty has done great things for me, and holy is his name. And his mercy is on those who fear him from generation to generation" (1:46-50).

Now the birth of Jesus Christ took place in this way. When his mother Mary had been betrothed to Joseph, before they came together she was found to be with child of the Holy Spirit; and her husband Joseph, being a just man and unwilling to put her to shame, resolved to divorce her quietly. But as he considered this, behold, an angel of the Lord appeared to him in a dream, saying, "Joseph, son of David, do not fear to take Mary your wife, for that which is conceived in her is of the Holy Spirit; she will bear a son, and you shall call his name Jesus, for he will save his people from their sins." All this took place to fulfill what the Lord had spoken by the prophet:
"Behold, a virgin shall conceive and bear a son,
    and his name shall be called Emmanuel"
(which means, God with us). When Joseph woke from sleep, he did as the angel of the Lord commanded him; he took his wife, but knew her not until she had borne a son; and he called his name Jesus.

Matt. 1:18-25

Chapter IV

The Stepfather of God

Matthew 1:18-25

Surely Joseph is the forgotten man of the nativity. Even the great artists of the world, many of whom have lavished their imagination upon this scene, have been content to make him a part of the dark background of their paintings. Yet this man was much more than such a piece of fleshly furniture. He was chosen to be "the stepfather of God."

The tradition followed by most artists has shown him to be an elderly man—strikingly so in comparison with the extreme youthfulness that the same tradition has attributed to Mary. The purpose of this, of course, was to make more reasonable the assertion that Joseph's marriage to Mary was never more than a Platonic relation, for the Mary cultists have not been content with the biblical teaching that she was a virgin mother but have given her the additional title "ever virgin." The Gospel references to Jesus' "brothers" and "sisters" (as in Matthew 13:55-

56) must then be disposed of by assuming that Joseph was an elderly widower with children. But all this is not history. It is mere legend, born from a desire to strengthen a false dogma.

Actually we know very little about Joseph. The genealogical table given in Matthew's Gospel relates that this carpenter had royal blood, for David was among his ancestors. That is an interesting fact, but it is hardly an important one. A little mathematics shows how many ancestors a person had twenty-eight generations ago. There would be over 268 million if there were no duplications. Even the humblest of us could find at least one illustrious forebear in such a multitude. What is important in considering Joseph is not his ancestry, but what he himself is.

What is great about this village carpenter that we should concern ourselves about him? Perhaps a sentence may serve as a window that will enable us to see him and his significance clearly: "He who has never profoundly doubted has never profoundly believed." Joseph's profound belief certainly followed some very profound doubts.

I

Certainly Joseph doubted profoundly. In part this was due to circumstances—in part, to his nature.

As might be expected of a man who worked with his hands, Joseph's mind took a practical, matter-of-fact turn. In modern terminology he was a "realist." He could never have composed a Magnificat, as Mary did. He had no vision, no ecstasies. His mind was trained to trust such things as measures, foot-rules, and weights. He knew what could and could not be done with certain materials, and he adjusted his plans accordingly. His approach to life was similar. Mysticism and poetry were suspect. Only with solid, unimaginative prose could he feel quite safe.

Such a man was called upon to believe the most unbelievable story ever told! It was shocking enough, in all conscience, that Mary, whom he had held in such high esteem and whose reputation had been spotless, should now confess herself to be pregnant. But didn't her "explanation" add insult to injury? How could she expect him to be so gullible, so naive? Doubtless many women, in comparable situations, had drawn freely on their imagination, but when had one presented such a transparent alibi as this? Joseph did know that he was free from responsibility for what had happened, but who then was guilty besides Mary?

It is plain from the biblical narrative that he did not believe Mary's story of an angelic announcement. Would we expect him to? Would we, if the same situation confronted us?

The only question was: What should he do about it? The tension is expressed in a sentence that tugs in two directions: "Being a just man and unwilling to put her to shame." As a dutiful son of the Law he knew the prescribed punishment for this violation of God's moral standard. She deserved death by stoning. But he loved her. He had already pledged her his lifelong affection and loyalty. He could not bear to think of such a terrible fate falling upon her. No matter what she had done, he loved her.

But did not another voice whisper, "Proclaim your own virtue by making a public condemnation of your fiancée's faithless conduct. Unless you do, people will certainly conclude that you are responsible for her condition, but that you were too much of a coward to face the consequences. Then the judgment of the community will fall upon you, even more than upon her." But even though he was sure that Mary had sinned grievously, he wanted to protect her from the result of her own folly and to shield her as far as possible from the vicious gossip of the village. She needed him now, more than ever before —even if she had lied to him.

After sleepless nights his conclusion was reached. He "resolved to divorce her privately." He would make no bid for public sympathy and no show of his own virtue. He would thus salvage at least part of his own dignity. Mary was a fortunate woman to be engaged to so understanding a man.

But this decision was not in accord with the plans of God. As a result, Joseph found his plans overturned just when he thought he had found a satisfying escape from his painful dilemma.

Exhausted by the struggle he had waged within his heart and contented with the solution he had found, Joseph fell asleep. In this sleep a divine messenger came to him with the word, "Joseph, son of David, do not fear to take Mary your wife, for that which is conceived in her is of the Holy Spirit; she will bear a son, and you shall call his name Jesus, for he will save his people from their sins." It may be noted, in passing, that here the most stupendous fact in all recorded history is announced as a reason why Joseph should carry out his marriage plans! This disproportion is incomprehensible, unless the historical accuracy of the story is accepted. Only such an A-bomb could have shattered Joseph's doubt.

II

But the doubt was shattered. The man who had "profoundly doubted" now became the man who "profoundly believed." In fact, there are few persons whom we meet in the records of our Lord's earthly life who held to such strong faith under such adverse circumstances.

True, he had had the angelic vision in a dream, but this was a fragile thing that was to withstand the battering of long years of inescapable doubtings. How brief a dream, and how long the years of testing, especially for a practical man like Joseph. Could one build a marriage successfully upon a dream? How could he ever be certain that this "vision" was not the feverish fulfillment of his wishes, the self-delusion of one who, in spite of all the evidence, still loves his fiancée? There is an earthly, peasant insight in "The Cherry Tree Carol" that is missing in our overromanticized thought. The expectant mother expresses the typical desires of her condition and asks, "Pluck me one cherry, Joseph, for I am with child." To which Joseph reacts with the biting anger of a jealous husband toward the unborn child: "Let him gather thee cherries that got thee with child."

Such plaguing doubts must certainly have recurred time and again during his working hours when his busy hands worked skillfully and unguided and his mind wrestled with uncertainty. The doubts probably also occurred during the long nights. The very presence of Jesus, later, and the contrast between this first-born of his wife and the children they had later been given, must have prodded his mind with doubt. Was the midnight word, "Do not fear to take Mary your wife, for that which is conceived in her is of the Holy Spirit," to be depended upon? Or should he believe the sly whisperings and lifted eyebrows of the villagers, who certainly had less elevated and more commonplace explanations to suggest?

We can be sure that there was gossip enough. Our certainty does not rest merely on the fact that human nature has not changed and that tongues then, as now, do not obey the laws of love, but also upon hints indirectly given in the biblical story. It is not hard to "read between the lines" of the bitter words of controversy recorded in John's Gospel: "They said to him, 'We were not born of fornication [as you were]; we have one Father [not a real one and a legal one, as you have]' " (8:41). The charge hurled later by Celsus, a vigorous critic of Christianity, that the record of a virgin birth was obvious nonsense and that the true father of Jesus was a centurion of the Roman army detachment stationed in Nazareth, may very well have been an echo of what the idle tongues of the village women had whispered.

Certainly Mary had to listen to these whispers also, and they must have cut deep into her sensitive spirit. This unique and blessed experience that was to bring grace to all men should not be so dragged into the mud by minds that delight in evil. In her first exultation of spirit she had spoken joyfully, "Behold, henceforth all generations will call me blessed; for he who is mighty has done great things for me, and holy is his name" (Luke 1:48-49). Instead, her own contemporaries had turned upon her with cutting tongues and had ridiculed her account of the supreme miracle of the ages. Yes, Mary had suffered.

But Mary *knew* that the accusations were untrue. No matter how reasonably the criticism might seem to be grounded, even though she also knew that premarital conception could have only a single explanation (except in this one instance), Mary had an assurance that not even her husband could share. For only she could *know* that she had not been guilty of illicit conduct. Her defense, within her own heart, did not need to rest upon the announcement of the angel Gabriel but upon her sure knowledge that she had not participated in sex relations with any man until after the birth of her first-born Son, when she and her husband began a normal marital relationship (Matt. 1:25).

This Joseph could never *know*. He had to build his married life upon trust—trust in the startling story of Mary and in her character and trust in the dream with its angelic visitor.

He could not even talk it over with someone else—certainly not with the villagers who showed so clearly that they regarded him as a sentimental fool. Not with Mary, for how could he do that without showing that his love for her was not strong enough to silence doubts? Could it be that this was the thing that caused him to turn for solace and security to the Old Testament Scriptures to see if there he might find some hint of that which Mary had told him? And might it not have been the fruit of this silent searching that resulted in the sentence that Matthew here injects into his story: "All this took place to fulfill what the Lord had spoken by the prophet: 'Behold, a virgin shall conceive and bear a son, and his name shall be called Emmanuel'" (which means, God with us)" (1:22-23)?

No one else has had to face Joseph's problem, so

we have no knowledge drawn from experience as to the way in which he met it. We cannot determine how he fed his faith and starved his doubts, but we can be sure of the fact itself. In the midst of profound doubt he still believed profoundly.

III

The fact that Joseph believed in the midst of doubt is one reason why he has a vital word to say to our generation. There are, to be sure, a few Mary spirits among us. There are still innocent, unquestioning, and obedient souls in whom Christ is born again with apparent ease. But such people are hardly characteristic of our century.

Most of us, like Joseph, have been educated to believe in things that we can touch and shape. We have confidence in the sequence of cause and effect. We order our lives by cool logic. We even boast of the fact that we are "realistic." In all this we are like Joseph, the carpenter of Nazareth.

We therefore find it hard to believe. Sometimes we even shrug off the effort. "Faith is a gift, like art or music," we say. "It is a matter of temperament, and mine just isn't the right kind. Christianity is all right for some people—in fact, sometimes I wish I had that kind of temperament, too. But it just isn't for me." Joseph might have spoken like that, but he did not. Such an attitude was fortunate for Mary, for the Child, and for Joseph himself.

The nativity story tells us that Jesus Christ is for all—for the matter-of-fact Josephs as truly as for the mystic Marys. To the latter he surely comes, in mingled ecstasy and pain. To the former the same Christ comes, quietly perhaps and with many a vigorous conflict with doubt. In either case, Christ comes with the same saving grace. The manner of his coming varies as greatly as human nature differs, but the thing to remember is that in every case his coming is real. Jesus is as vital, as wonderful, and as eternal to the Josephs among us as to the Marys. And Joseph's acceptance was a miracle as truly as was Mary's conception.

Joseph was an ordinary man. Like Mary, he illustrates the truth of the Apostle's word: "God chose what is low and despised in the world, even things that are not, to bring to nothing things that are, so that no human being might boast in the presence of God" (1 Cor. 1:28-29). By that choice of God, Joseph ceased to be an ordinary man.

A few years ago, when our family was to leave for a period of overseas service in a Europe shadowed by the threat of renewed war, we made plans for the possibility that our children would be cared for in case something should happen to their parents. Knowing that such a responsibility would not be a light one, we had considerable hesitance about asking a friend for permission to designate him to serve in such a capacity. His immediate response to our telephone request was, "Certainly, I am highly honored that you should have such confidence in us that you are willing to entrust your children to our care." It was such a honor that God conferred on Joseph! It was important, surely, that the earthly mother of the eternal Son of God should be chosen with care. It was equally important that his stepfather be carefully selected. Not every man could have served as stepfather for God's Son. For this responsible task, God chose Joseph.

To God's tribute we must join the one Jesus himself paid to Joseph's memory. We do not know how long Joseph lived, but the silence of the Gospels suggests strongly that he died during Jesus' youth. His last appearance in the pages of Scripture is when the boy was twelve. After Jesus' ministry began at the age of thirty, there are references only to Mary and to their children. But whether or not the years of association were many, Joseph's character, strength, love, and tenderness made a lasting impression. When, in later years, Jesus sought a human relationship that might serve to picture the character and nature of God, he used the word "Father."

Could there be a higher tribute paid to this simple carpenter, who was called to serve as the stepfather of God?

*In those days a decree went out from Caesar
Augustus that all the world should be enrolled. This
was the first enrollment, when Quirinius was gover-
nor of Syria. And all went to be enrolled, each to his
own city. And Joseph also went up from Galilee, from
the city of Nazareth, to Judea, to the city of David,
which is called Bethlehem, because he was of the
house and lineage of David, to be enrolled with
Mary his betrothed, who was with child.*

Luke 2:1-5

*When Herod the king heard this, he was troubled,
and all Jerusalem with him; and assembling all the
chief priests and scribes of the people, he inquired
of them where the Christ was to be born. They told
him, "In Bethlehem of Judea; for so it is written
by the prophet:*

*" 'And thou Bethlehem, in the land of Judah,
art by no means least among the rulers of Judah;
for from thee shall come a ruler
who will govern my people Israel.' "*

Matt. 2:3-6

Chapter V

The Royal Servant

Luke 2:1-6, Matthew 2:3-6

What manner of child is this that an emperor serves as a mere stagehand to set up the scenery for his birth? How amused the mighty emperor Caesar Augustus would have been had he known that some obscure subjects in a distant province should have dared picture him in this light. Granted even the keenest of foresight, he would have ridiculed the notion that in centuries to come men would remember him best because he, humanly speaking, was responsible for the birth of the Babe in Bethlehem "to fulfill what the Lord had spoken by the prophet."

The great Correggio has given the world a significant painting, "The Holy Night," in which he dramatizes the startling truth of Christmas. Every person he portrays, from the greatest to the humblest, from the joyful parents to the cattle in the stall, are seen only by the light that shines from the Babe who lies in the manger. All men borrow their glory from him to whom alone all glory truly belongs: Augustus, because he unknowingly ordered a census in a small, unruly province; Pilate, because for a moment the prisoner stood before him and was condemned to death; Nero, Domitian, and Julian the Apostate, who sought to use their regal might to stamp out the life of the early Christian community. Only this contact, negative though it was, with Jesus of Nazareth has prevented their name and fame from vanishing into the gloom that has swallowed the world's mightiest men.

I

The first truth that is reinforced by the Gospel account is the necessity that confronts every man of being God's tool.

That is to say, every man, no matter how unknowing or rebellious he may be of God and his will, cannot avoid doing the task that God's wisdom and grace have prescribed for him. Here there is no option. However much our human pride may rebel against this truth, it remains true. God is no beggar, humbly beseeching our indispensable cooperation. He is the Lord. "God said, Let there be . . . and there was" (Gen. 1:3). He is sovereign over the stubborn matter of his creation and over man, its climax. Man has no choice but to fulfill the Master's will. He is a tool, whether he wills it or not.

The great prophets of Judah knew this. Jeremiah,

for example, was commanded to wear thongs and a yoke upon his neck while he said to the envoys of the kings of Edom, Moab, Tyre, and Sidon, "Thus says the Lord of hosts, the God of Israel: This is what you shall say to your masters: 'It is I who by my great power and my outstretched arm have made the earth, with the men and animals that are on the earth, and I give it to whomever it seems right to me. Now I have given all these lands into the hand of Nebuchadnezzar, the king of Babylon, my servant, and I have given him also the beasts of the field to serve him. All the nations shall serve him and his son and his grandson, until the time of his own land comes; then many nations and great kings shall make him their slave'" (Jer. 27:4-7). God is the Lord, even over the greatest of kings and kingdoms, whether they believe in him or not.

There is no basis in Scripture for the well-intentioned but essentially blasphemous suggestion we hear even in the church: "God depends upon you, your willingness and talents." That may flatter our egos, but it is not true. That God *wants* us is grandly true, but he does not *need* us. His purposes of judgment and grace will be accomplished in us and through us whether we wish and intend it or not. God can write straight even with crooked lines.

In his Small Catechism Martin Luther carefully guards against an impious misinterpretation of Jesus' words in the model prayer by saying: "God's name certainly is holy in itself. . . . God's kingdom comes indeed without our praying for it. . . . The good and gracious will of God is surely done without our prayer, but we ask in this prayer that it may be done also among us."

A particularly clear statement of this divine sovereignty is found in Isaiah 45. Here the prophet dares to apply to a pagan ruler the hopeful and anticipated title of "The Anointed—the Messiah." Cyrus, the Persian king, plans to release the Hebrew inhabitants of Babylon, after their long and lonely years of captivity. So the prophet cries out: "Thus says the Lord to his anointed, to Cyrus, whose right hand I have grasped, to subdue nations before him . . . : I will go before you and level the mountains, I will break in pieces the doors of bronze and cut asunder the bars of iron, . . . that you may know that it is I, the Lord, the God of Israel, who call you by your name." As though to anticipate protests, ancient and modern, the prophetic words continue: "I surname you, though you do not know me . . . . I gird you, though you do not know me, that men may know, from the rising of the sun and from the west, that there is none besides me; I am the Lord, and there is no other" (vv. 1-6).

Seldom have words so encompassed the truth of God's absolute sovereignty over man as these have: "Woe to him who strives with his Maker, an earthen vessel with the potter! Does the clay say to him who fashions it, 'What are you making'? or 'Your work has no handles'? Woe to him who says to a father, 'What are you begetting?' or to a woman, 'With what are you in travail?' Thus says the Lord, the Holy One of Israel, and his Maker: 'Will you question me about my children, or command me concerning the work of my hands?' " (vv. 9-11).

God has pledged his word from of old. His Son was to be born in Bethlehem of Judea. But since the expectant mother was in Galilee, "a decree went out from Caesar Augustus," in order that the promise could be carried out. The stage had to be set, even if it required a pagan emperor to do it.

Frankly, it is impossible for our minds to reconcile the two biblically asserted facts of God's absolute sovereignty and man's responsibility. Can a Pilate or a Caiaphas, even a Judas Iscariot, be held responsible for crucifying a guiltless man if their actions were essential for the fulfillment of God's will? Human minds have always struggled with this dilemma, as is clearly evidenced in the bewilderment of the disciples when their Lord spoke to them of his approaching betrayal and death. He "answered" this dilemma only with the paradoxical assertion, "The Son of man goes as it is written of him, but woe to that man by whom the Son of man is betrayed! It would have been better for that man if he had not been born" (Matt. 26:24). That Peter had learned to accept, if not to understand, this dual truth is evident from his words on the day of Pentecost: "This Jesus, delivered up according to the definite plan and foreknowledge of God, you crucified and killed by the hands of lawless men. . . . Save yourselves from this crooked generation" (Acts 2:23, 40).

Is it not important for all men to know that God's purposes cannot be frustrated? All the schemes and wickedness of men are powerless to block his gracious purposes. Instead, as contrary winds drive a sailboat toward its desired goal, so does the evil of men, whether they are ignorant of him or arrogantly presume themselves to be "the masters of their fate," serve to effect God's will for mankind. What can a Khrushchev or a Mao hope to do to block the plans of him who arranged for Augustus to have a child born in Bethlehem?

Evil is never excused or lightly treated, but encouragement is given to those who must bear the bitterness and pain. With Joseph, sold into Egyptian slavery by his brothers, they can still say confidently to their persecutors, "As for you, you meant evil against me; but God meant it for good, to bring it about that many people should be kept alive" (Gen. 50:20). It was such a conviction that caused Paul to write, "We know that in everything God works for good with those who love him, who are called according to his purpose. . . . If God is for us, who is against us?" (Rom. 8:28, 31). Even the ill-disposed Caesars of earthly power are tools in his great hand!

Yet an important point must be noted. This is a truth asserted by William Temple when he was Archbishop of York, in a sermon preached in St. Paul's Cathedral of London: "While we deliberate, he reigns. While we decide wisely, he reigns. While we decide foolishly, he reigns. When we serve him in humble loyalty, he reigns. When we serve him self-assertedly, he reigns. When we rebel and seek to withhold our service, he reigns." No man can avoid being a tool in the strong hand of God, but he can choose, voluntarily, to be something wonderfully more.

II

God offers every man the joyful possibility of being his servant. A tool has no option but to do its owner's will; a servant gives himself to his master voluntarily. The necessity is laid upon the shoulders of every man; only obedient believers are granted the joyful privilege.

The Lord Jesus tells us this truth in slightly different words, the meaning of which our translations unfortunately do not clearly reveal: "You are my friends if you do what I command you. No longer do I call you servants [literally "slaves"], for the servant [slave] does not know what his master is doing; but I have called you friends, for all that I have heard from my Father I have made known to you" (John 15:14-15). The slave is a mere "breathing tool" with no will of his own; the friend offers free and loving cooperation. It is this second possibility that our Savior opens before us when he calls us into his fellowship of grace and service.

We may easily fail to understand the significance

of that moment in our worship in American churches when we place money upon the altar. Sometimes
we even think of the offering as a secular and unwelcome intrusion into a spiritual mood. We forget
that these financial gifts are symbolic of a larger and
more inclusive thankoffering, one that is vividly revealed in an incident in a tiny Liberian village a
generation ago. The missionary had preached fervently on "The Blessedness of Giving" and the small
congregation joined lustily in an offertory hymn.
Men and women in colorful homespun robes brought
gourds of palm oil, bunches of cassava, rice, plantains, and even cackling chickens. Last of all came
Boymah, a leper, hobbling painfully up the aisle,
empty-handed. Lowering the large wooden bowl,
that had been used to receive the offerings of believers, Boymah climbed into it himself. Having no
earthly possessions, he was offering himself. Unless
our gifts have, undergirding them, this final gift,
they are not acceptable to God.

The feeble response of our churches to the worldwide mission of evangelism and mercy in a desperately needed world is abundant evidence of the
fact that this total self-commitment has not been
made. Perhaps that is why the "pocketbook protection" that fund raisers talk about is so strong. The
lay preacher of Spurgeon's day, Billy Bray, spoke
to us, as truly as to his own generation, when he said
accusingly: "In some o' our chapels, the folks collect
old rags and bones and sell them to raise missionary

money. Some collect old clo'es an' old shoes, and have a jumble-sale. I don't think it's right to give the Lord old rags and bones. The Lord deserves the best, and he shall have the best. An old wumman promised me a goose for my new chapel. She promised to sell every tenth goose o' her flock an' give the money to the Lord. But whut d'you think she done? When she found a bit of a chick that was likely to die, she'd put it in an old stockin' and lay it by the fire, and say, 'If that chick lives, I'll give it to missions.' I know an old wumman down at St. Just, an' when the Lord tried her faith and let one o' the geese die, she said, 'What a pity! That un wor the missionary goose!'"

What he was combatting was the still-prevalent notion that we are called upon to supply a motive from the outside that is strong enough to overcome a man's reluctance to surrender what he regards as his own property. Sales, dances, bazaars, and other projects are supposed to offer something in exchange for the money their promoters seek to gain from "givers." A columnist categorized the attempt like this: "Churches and charitable organizations run illegal (or legal) gambling because that's where the sure way of getting money for holy causes from people who wouldn't otherwise contribute if the Almighty pushed a .45 at them." The fundamental criticism that must be made of all such programs— and of many that are less crass—is that nothing glorifies God and is acceptable to him unless the motive that prompts the action is thankful love. That is why stewardship must begin with rebirth.

A man may go through all the motions of obedient service and yet be far removed in spirit from him whom he serves. The often-overlooked elder prodigal in our Lord's parable (Luke 15:25-32) illustrates this. He behaved like a loving son, but his real attitude was that of a hired servant, asking always, "What will I get out of this?" If the younger brother stands under judgment, before his repentance, because he was prodigal of his own inheritance, how much more does this smug and critical older brother deserve the name "prodigal" for being wasteful of something even more precious, his father's love? God does not seek our obedience, merely, but a love of which obedience is one of the fruits.

To serve as a co-worker with God, to be his willing servant, is no burdensome obligation, but a joyful privilege. Donald Grey Barnhouse told, after the Korean War, of his visit to a refugee congregation in Pusan. It worshiped in three tattered army tents placed end to end. It was surrounded by flimsy refugee shacks. After a Thanksgiving service the congregation of 600 adults contributed an amazing $225. "How in the world did your people manage to raise that much?" asked the surprised visitor. "Well, nearly all of them were shopkeepers or workers of some kind in Pyongyang. When they came here just a year ago this month, they began to pick up any jobs at all that were available and some were able to start in little by little to buy and sell things. As a result, none are now on government relief. When the time came for the offering they counselled together and said, 'When we came here a year ago we had empty hands and nothing but the clothes we wore on our backs. The Lord has seen us through the past year and blessed us mightily. Let us show our gratitude to him by giving him everything we have and starting again in faith tomorrow with empty hands, being perfectly confident that he will see us through the year that lies ahead.' With that spirit the offering was taken." This incident recalls, doesn't it, the delightful astonishment of the Apostle Paul at the generous spirit of the believers in Macedonia: "In a severe test of affliction, their abundance of joy and their extreme poverty have overflowed in a wealth of liberality on their part. For they gave according to their means, as I can testify, and beyond their means, of their own free will, begging us earnestly for the favor of taking part . . . ." The key, then as now, is found in the next words, "First they gave themselves to the Lord" (2 Cor. 8:2-5).

The compulsion is from within. Clarence C. Stoughton, who did so much to enable the church of our day to understand this, has said, "Christian stewardship is believing in Jesus Christ, obeying him. It is surrendering my life to him, because I know him and trust him and am everlastingly thankful to him. . . . Such giving of myself—including my time, my talents, my prayers, my money—will be as natural as the shining of the sun or the fruiting of a good tree. No one need compel it. Because I know that he is my Lord who redeemed me with his death on the cross, I cannot help but be his, live under him in his kingdom and serve him in everlasting righteousness and blessedness. No compulsion, other than my gratitude." As G. K. Chesterton once phrased it, "He who is conscious of a debt that he can never repay will be forever paying it." We do owe that kind of debt!

Caesar Augustus knew nothing of all this, so we can scarcely scorn him for playing only a menial role of a tool in the hands of the Lord God. Relatively at least, he had no alternative. But we can choose —not whether or not God's will shall be done, for here we and all men are powerless, but we can choose the high dignity and the rewarding satisfaction of voluntarily permitting him to use us, wherever and in what manner he thinks best.

Tool or servant—it must be one or the other. Which will you choose to be?

And in that region there were shepherds out in the field, keeping watch over their flock by night. And an angel of the Lord appeared to them, and the glory of the Lord shone around them, and they were filled with fear. And the angel said to them, "Be not afraid; for behold, I bring you good news of a great joy which will come to all the people; for to you is born this day in the city of David a Savior, who is Christ the Lord. And this will be a sign for you: you will find a babe wrapped in swaddling cloths and lying in a manger." And suddenly there was with the angel a multitude of the heavenly host praising God and saying,
"Glory to God in the highest,
and on earth peace among men with whom he is pleased!"

Luke 2:8-14

Chapter VI

The Common Man

Luke 2:8-20

How simple is the scene described! And how shocking! Its appeal is to the romantic mind of a child, but our adult sophistication insists upon "reasonable" questions: If God wanted to capture the world for himself, why should the world's Redeemer have been born in an out-of-the-way provincial village? Why not Rome or, at the very least, Jerusalem? Every one who is engaged in public relations knows that if you want to reach vast numbers of men, you must set up office in a great city like New York. Why should God have ignored so simple a fact of life? Bethlehem!

And *shepherds*. Even in a small country town there were some important people, especially when it was swollen with visitors drawn by an imperial decree. And Jerusalem was only a half dozen miles away. If God's heavenly messengers were to proclaim the best news that the world has ever heard, why weren't they more selective about their audience?

Yet who are we to predetermine what God must do?

I

God wanted to make it clear that he is greatly concerned about ordinary people. That ought to interest us because that is what we are, the vast majority of us. As Lincoln put it, "God must have loved the common people—he made so many of them!" And it was to them that the first announcement of the Savior's birth was made.

The great Boston preacher, Phillips Brooks, once asserted: "The exceptional people, the millionaires and the paupers, the sages and the fools, the saints and the scoundrels, are the capes and promontories which jut out into the sea and thus become conspicuous." But Charles R. Brown, who quotes this in *The Gospel for Main Street,* adds, "The great continent of human life is made up of average people who have two talents apiece. They are the backbone of any nation."

That may be true, but most of us don't really believe it. Our newspapers presumably know what their readers think important, so it becomes front-page news when the wife of the President of the United States stumbles on a Greek ruin and slightly turns her ankle. If you and I were to fall and break our necks, the fact would perhaps be noted on page 16. Most present-day leaders of men, aware of future elections, would hesitate to speak as bluntly as Napoleon who, when he was reminded that a proposed campaign might cost the lives of thousands of French youth, wrote them off as "superfluous people." But in spite of their caution, they still act on the bland assumption that masses of men are "expendable."

Sometimes even religious leaders agree. That was the real point at issue when John the Baptist questioned whether the Man of Nazareth was indeed what he thought him to be. If he was in fact the promised Messiah, why didn't he get about his real and important business instead of frittering away his time and energy on lame peasants and blind beggars? (Matt. 11:2-6). It was perhaps natural that Jesus' forerunner should have felt like that. Both the Sadducees and the Pharisees had outspoken contempt for the mass of men, whom they called "the men of the earth." They even questioned whether such men could properly be regarded as "children of Abraham" and heirs of the promises God had given, for how could they know, much less obey, the thousands of applications that the scribes had derived from the Law of Moses? In their opinion, also, Jesus paid altogether too much attention to such common folk. "This man receives sinners and eats with them" (Luke 15:2).

But not only do leaders of men fail to accept the ordinary man as important—he often doesn't even claim such importance for himself. He has only one vote, so why bother? He is a stranger in the anthill of the great city, and no Mrs. Grundy will be watching to check up on his behavior, so why not wander a bit from the accustomed path? He is the small investor in a large corporation who acknowledges no responsibility for its policies so long as his dividend check comes promptly. He is the man on the assembly-line who is as interchangeable as the parts he assembles. He is the passive church member, prepared to criticize those who assume responsibility but never taking it himself. He is, said Jesus, a "wicked and slothful servant" (Matt. 25:26) because he has convinced himself that he is quite unimportant.

But God thinks otherwise. And so the glorious news was proclaimed to humble working men rather than to the religious and economic aristocrats in Jerusalem.

Mary's words of praise had forecast this revolutionary approach:

"He has . . . exalted those of low degree;

he has filled the hungry with good things,

and the rich he has sent empty away" (Luke 1:52-53).

And later James, struggling against obvious partiality for the rich in the early church (how little things have changed!), writes, "Has not God chosen those who are poor in the world to be rich in faith and heirs of the kingdom which he has promised to those who love him?" (James 2:5).

From the first preaching of the Gospel it has been

most readily and gladly received by simple, ordinary people. It was so in our Lord's own ministry: "I thank thee, Father, Lord of heaven and earth, that thou hast hidden these things from the wise and understanding and revealed them to babes" (Matt. 11:25). He knew that "the common people heard him gladly" (Mark 12:37, KJV). This was true also of the ministry of his most effective apostle, for what Paul wrote to the Corinthians might well have been repeated in other cities where he had established congregations: "For consider your call, brethren; not many of you were wise according to worldly standards, not many were powerful, not many were of noble birth; but God chose what is foolish in the world to shame the wise, God chose what is weak in the world to shame the strong, God chose what is low and despised in the world, even things that are not, to bring to nothing things that are" (1 Cor. 1: 26-28). This has been true ever since in every part of the world. Coolies, outcasts, peasants, and lepers are the first to come. It is easier by far to reach the "down and outs" than the "up and outs."

Why? Because the major obstacle to the Gospel is pride. That is why Jesus found his most unyielding opposition among the wealthy, aristocratic Sadducees and the devout, middle-class Pharisees. That is why contemporary religious cults that soft-pedal the message of divine grace, but substitute some pattern of work-righteousness, are so strong in their appeal to the upper strata of society. That is why careful ob-

servers have found so much to criticize in the program of the status-conscious suburban congregation
which too often has merely substituted meritorious
service at the annual bazaar for the penitential demands of the Roman Church.

Men are not turned aside from such face-saving
forms of religion by the harshness of its demands
upon their time, money, and energy, if only they are
permitted to salvage their self-respect. This pride is
why the natural man is a born enemy of the Gospel.
That is why our Lord spoke so shockingly of the fact
that "the tax-collectors and the harlots go into the
kingdom of God before you" (the priests and elders)
(Matt. 21:31).

But there are people, like the "men of the earth"
who tended their sheep on Bethlehem's hills that
night, who have little self-respect to lose. They are
already overwhelmed by their own self-despisings.
They have no illusions about themselves.

To such men, the unknown and unremembered
of earth's history, the revelation of God's unfathom-
able, utterly undeserved grace comes and is joyfully
received. " 'Let us go over to Bethlehem and see this
thing that has happened, which the Lord has made
known to us.' And they went with haste."

II

What happens when such ordinary men encounter
God? The answer does not concern the shepherds

only, for it concerns each of us when, in church or elsewhere, we hear God's Good News directed at us —"Be not afraid . . . for to you is born this day in the city of David a Savior, who is Christ the Lord." The circumstances may indeed be less dramatic and the messenger all too human, but the confrontation and the message are unchanged.

Perhaps Luther's words, addressed to a congregation in Torgau in 1523, summarize what took place then—and always: "True worship consists of this: that our dear Lord himself speaks to us through his holy Word and we reply to him in prayer and hymns of praise." The meeting of God and man, then, results in a dialogue, a conversation.

Yet in this dialogue it is always God who first addresses man. Biblical religion is very emphatic on this point. It says nothing about "men of mystical bent of mind" who have "a genius for religion." It always begins with a God who often catches man quite unaware, as he did Moses in the wilderness or the shepherds in the fields. God comes to seek and to save the lost. The initiative is wholly his.

Have you been alert to note this fact as it is expressed in the historic liturgy of Western Christendom? The worshiper, having entered the holy place through the narrow gate of confession and repentance, hears the majestic voice of God speak to him through that part of the service known as "the Office of the Word." This includes the Scripture lessons read from the Old Testament, the Epistles, and the

Gospels. Their truth is then packaged in either the Nicene or the Apostles' Creed. After this it is explained and applied to our contemporary situation by the sermon. All this corresponds to the angelic announcement heard by the shepherds long ago. God's Word to us establishes our conversation.

How tragic if we do not receive this divine address with joy and fervid anticipation! Yet, as someone has said, there are some people in church who look like guests at a royal banquet who couldn't afford to be left out, but who have been forbidden by their doctor to eat anything.

Such spiritual dyspepsia may be due to the fact that we have forgotten that God is our gracious host or, possibly, to the fact that we have forgotten that his food is not given to us to admire but to eat. His speech, in other words, is not a monologue but is intended to call forth a response from us. Isn't this the heartfelt wish of every lover?

> *He looked at her as a lover can;*
> *She looked at him as one who awakes.*
>
> Browning

Our worship service does not end when God has spoken to his people. Instead, it continues with the offering of our grateful love, a sort of down-payment of the continuing dedication of ourselves we intend to offer to him as "a living sacrifice." This is expressed in the Offertory, in which we sing of this dedication, and the Prayer of the Church, where we blend our wills and petitions with those of our Lord.

All this implies, certainly, that our worship does not end when the organ notes fade away. That usher was certainly right who, when approached by a late-comer who arrived at the door just at the benediction to ask, "Oh, is the service over?" replied quickly, "No, our service is just beginning."

We misunderstand the nature and purpose of our coming together as believers if we think of it as an hour during which we are entitled to be entertained by the minister and the choir. Rather we ought to view such an experience as parallel to the briefing sessions given our aviators during the war. Men came to learn the objective of the next raid and the means by which it could be accomplished successfully. When they left the briefing rooms it was not to gather in groups to discuss the eloquence (or lack of it) of the officers in charge, but to get into their planes and streak off to achieve their assignment.

From Denmark comes Søren Kierkegaard's fable of the geese that is still a challenge to every worshiper. Suppose, he said, that geese could talk. They might then arrange it so that they would gather together every seventh day. Each Sunday one of the ganders would mount the fence and preach to his fellow geese about the lofty destiny geese had, the high goal that the Creator had set before them and how, by the use of their wings, they might fly away to distant regions where they were truly meant to live. This happened every week, but after the assembly broke up, each goose would waddle home and eat the grain the farmer had scattered. That was the end of it until the next Sunday.

By Monday the geese were ready to tell each other what terrible things would happen if they took the Sunday message seriously. They spoke of one who *had* made full use of the wings that the Creator had given him and of the awful fate that had befallen him. And so, Sunday after Sunday, they gathered together in solemn assembly, but during the week they were content to remain in the barnyard. There they grew plump and delicate—just right to be eaten on the next holiday.

The shepherds were wiser. After the thrilling visit of the angels had ended, they said to one another, "Let us go over to Bethlehem and see this thing that has happened, which the Lord has made known to us." They went with haste to find Mary and Joseph and the Babe. Then, realizing, as every man must who takes seriously the glorious announcement of divine mercy, that this gift was far too great to be enclosed in their small lives alone, "they made known the saying which had been told them concerning this child."

The possibility of great things is present when God meets ordinary people—like us.

Now there was a man in Jerusalem, whose name was Simeon, and this man was righteous and devout, looking for the consolation of Israel, and the Holy Spirit was upon him. And it had been revealed to him by the Holy Spirit that he should not see death before he had seen the Lord's Christ. And inspired by the Spirit he came into the temple; and when the parents brought in the child Jesus, to do for him according to the custom of the law, he took him up in his arms and blessed God and said,

"Lord, now lettest thou thy servant depart in peace, according to thy word;

for mine eyes have seen thy salvation

which thou hast prepared in the presence of all peoples,

a light for revelation to the Gentiles,

and for glory to thy people Israel."

Luke 2:25-32

Chapter VII

The Satisfied Worshiper

Luke 2:22-38

Even those whose reading has not extended beyond the pages of newspapers and magazines know something of the interesting discoveries that have been made in the Jordan wilderness. The recovery of a still-increasing supply of ancient documents, buried by devout but sectarian Jews just before the final Roman invasion of Palestine, which resulted in the capture and destruction of Jerusalem in 70 A.D., has cast significant light on religious life of Palestine in a period that was roughly identical with that of the ministries of John the Baptist and our Lord.

Among other things, they reinforce our knowledge that there existed, in that day, a considerable number of people who were looking forward, expectantly and hopefully, to the coming of God's Messiah, the Christ, who had been promised with increasing clarity throughout the centuries of Hebrew history. In a singular and supreme sense he would be "the anointed one" of God, sent to accomplish his ultimate purpose and to establish his kingdom.

Our text introduces us to two such people. Simeon and Anna. We know very little about either of them as individuals, but they are, in some sense, symbolic of this eager company. A few scraps of information are given us about Anna, although the data given is rather difficult to unravel, since there is some question as to the precise meaning of the phrases that Luke uses regarding her. But of Simeon, with whom we are now particularly concerned, we are told nothing at all. We do not even know his age, although artists' attempts to portray this scene show him as an old man. Whether this results from the fact that Anna was an old woman and that Simeon's story is told in close connection with hers, or whether it is merely the apparent willingness of Simeon to die after having found in Jesus the fulfillment of his hopes, I do not know. In any event, tradition has pictured him thus.

Yet this is not necessarily correct. A man might well achieve the climax of his life's hopes while he is still in his twenties, so that all that happens thereafter becomes a sort of anticlimax. That might well have been true of Simeon. All we can say with certainty is that this man was in the temple as the Child was brought there, when his parents came to offer the sacrifice demanded by Moses' law. Simeon welcomed this humble group with words that are often used in the liturgy of the church: "Lord, now lettest thou thy servant depart in peace, according to thy word; for mine eyes have seen thy salvation which thou hast prepared in the presence of all peoples, a light for revelation to the Gentiles, and for glory to thy people Israel."

I

The first thing that Simeon tells us concerning God's gift to men is that it is the gift of a full life.

Simeon's own life was climaxed in that moment when God's salvation, long promised by the ancient prophets, was made known unto him. Whether Simeon was old or young, he had always had abundant reason to be thankful to God, as we all have. He had been granted innumerable blessings, but most of them he—like us probably—took for granted, simply because he had always had them. Such everyday gifts as those of sight and taste are accepted matter-of-factly. How much they enrich life we discover only when, if only for a brief time, they are lost to us. Having them, we use them day after day, without any thought of God's mercy in having given them to us. One might almost say that we scarcely use these gifts, because we so rarely see or taste or hear what God has granted us. In a certain sense our carelessness robs us of the mercies so freely given us by God.

Sometimes we even think to demonstrate how "religious" we are by de-emphasizing and denying God's material, everyday blessings. In every century there have been those who have tried to exalt the "spiritual" at the expense of the "material" side of life. Such people seem to think that piety demands the rejection of many of the normal experiences that life offers us. I once visited a Trappist monastery, where I saw such a philosophy of life put into practice. The monks slept on wooden benches, with only a single blanket to cover them against bitter, midwestern winters and with no mattress but a thin pad. These Trappists got up long before daylight and padded into an unheated chapel for the day's first period of formal devotion. In addition to the traditional monkish vows of poverty, chastity, and obedience they had taken the vow of silence, refusing to use in normal conversation the tongues that God had given them. I could only admire the courage and self-control with which they had slammed the door on so many of the earthly blessings that are showered upon us in abundance. But I could not escape an insistent doubt about their undertaking. They did these things as a service of dedication to God, but at the same time they seemed to be denying the goodness of God's creation.

Unfortunately, so much of our religious life—Protestant as well as Roman Catholic—is tainted with such a negative attitude toward the things of this world. So frequently we try to prove that we are truly devout by rejecting many of the healthy and wholesome pleasures of this life. That is why so many think of religion always in negative terms, a long list of "Thou shalt nots." Does this adequately express

God's will? Would it not be more truly biblical to say that God has given us all these earthly pleasures to use in accordance with his gracious purpose? Each pleasure ought to be a little window through which we can see the splendor of God's great gift of love.

For years we have had hanging in a window of our home in the Advent season a transparency showing a German village in midwinter. Each year our children have opened a tiny door, and as it swung on its hinge, we could see another joy of Christmas —a doll, a wooden block, a ball, a tree ornament. But what have they to do with Advent and Christmas— and with the Gift? Of course the climactic act comes on December 25, when the largest and central door is thrown open to reveal the holy family. But we need to be made ready for this manifestation of grace. We must have time to prepare ourselves, through the commonplaces of life, for the tremendous and vital thing that each Christmas proclaims.

All of life's significant experiences need such preparation. Visitors in Dresden's famed Zwinger, in the days before the last war, found themselves, for example, passing through one room after another, each crowded with the artistic treasures of centuries. Suddenly, to their surprise, they entered a small room with quite bare walls. The reason became clear only when they passed into the next room and found themselves confronting the "Sistine Madonna." It was as though the curators of that gallery realized that visitors needed a brief pause in their viewing, that the impressions made on eye and mind by other paintings should be momentarily erased in order that this supreme treasure of the Dresden gallery might be seen with freshened vision. If that is true of such a physical object as Raphael's masterpiece, how much more is this true of the miracle of God's Gift that Christmas celebrates?

Life's lesser, homely joys may serve just such a purpose. They can be little windows through which we can get fresh glimpses of the wonderful fact of God's love, a love that we see fully and completely in Jesus the Christ. There is, admittedly, a certain danger involved. We may become so absorbed in the wonder of these material blessings that we never look beyond them to the Giver. That often happens to people at Christmastime. They become so engrossed in the gifts that surround the tree, those they receive and those they have given, that they forget God's gift of his Son. This is indeed a genuine threat to our spiritual health. In the ancient petition of the Litany we must still pray, "In all time of our prosperity, good Lord, deliver us." Yet, though these lesser blessings from God may be a means of temptation, they are nonetheless part of God's dealing with men. We ought to be aware of and thankful for God's goodness in filling life with abundant joys. How empty life would be, how almost meaningless, apart from the gifts of family and home, husband, wife and children, and purposeful labor. How good of God to bless us with these human associations that magnify life's joys and greatly diminish its sorrows. It is precisely because of the importance of these matters that the church cautions and seeks to aid its youth in making marital choices thoughtfully. We must live with these human associations for a long time. To recognize this is to take a positive view of life, to accept joyfully the fullness of life that is God's gift in the relationship of the sexes.

The same is true of our labor. Many of us are, to be sure, a bit like children who, no matter how they really like school, still feel compelled to bow to the convention of shouting, "Oh, it's vacation time! School is over!" Parents know how quickly these same children will be bored with play and how they will look forward to the resumption of school, though the admission is rarely permitted to pass their lips. But aren't we adults much like that with regard to our work? We talk about how wonderful it will be when our vacation weeks come around or when, after retirement, our lives will become an unending vacation. Yet we need not have a wide acquaintance among those who have passed retirement age to know that for many "the bottom dropped out of life" when meaningful work ceased. We need to be engaged in some activity that makes a contribution, however small, to the welfare of the society within which we live, even if it is nothing more than providing the material needs of our immediate loved ones, for whom God has given us special responsibility. Work, too, is one of God's blessed gifts.

Yet, overarching all material blessings is God's supreme gift: "Mine eyes have seen thy salvation which thou hast prepared in the presence of all peoples." The spiritual blessings of God are eternal and therefore more important than even the greatest of the temporal blessings we have received. These include a Savior who speaks to us the word of forgiveness and life, a Father who will never leave or forsake us, a Comforter and Strengthener who upholds us every moment with his boundless resources. How shall we measure the greatness of this Christmas Gift?

How precious the gift of worship with its opportunity to enter into the presence of the Most High, that he may speak his life-giving Word to us and that we may address him with our thankful prayers and hymns! How privileged we are that the doors of our churches are open and that we can come. Associated with this is the gift of the Sacrament of the Supper. How right Martin Luther was when in the preface to his *Small Catechism* he commented that if Christians really understood the vital contribution that this Sacrament makes to their spiritual well-being they would go to their pastors and say, "We insist that you give the Sacrament to us more frequently." Four or five times a year, suggested Luther, would be an absolute minimum. Yet in the average American congregation almost half of our "members" fail to come to the Communion table even once in twelve months. And many who do qualify as "communing members" come only once or twice. Does this mean that we think ourselves so good, so spiritually mature, that we do not need God's gracious gift for future growth? Or does it mean only that we do not think at all?

Simeon did think and he rejoiced in every gift that God granted him, whether material or spiritual. With words and life he blessed God that he had been given a full life.

II

Because Simeon was aware that God had given him a full life, he dared look forward confidently to a peaceful death.

The funeral practices of modern America reveal clearly that we do not like to think about death, even when its cold hand reaches into and disrupts the family circle. We place the corpse, carefully rouged, on a satin pillow, in the midst of mountains of flowers. While soothing music is piped into the room we say, not that he has died, but "passed away," "is no longer with us," or "has gone to his reward." We have come a long way from the day when it was the sad responsibility of the deceased family to shape the coffin, dig the grave, and shovel back the dirt, and we are not going to return to it. Yet is it not true that every man, from the moment of his birth, is stricken with a fatal disease—life? The death rate of humanity continues to stand at one hundred per cent. Secular writers know it, even if the church is silent, and they choose such titles as "Dark at the Head of the Stairs" and "Long Day's Journey into Night." Even Clarence Darrow wondered at the "general conspiracy to keep silent about that even which awaits us all." Is not Paul Tillich right when he suggests that death is not merely the scissors that sever the thread of life, but rather a thread woven into the very fabric of our existence?

Someone said recently, "Life really begins when a person first realizes how soon it ends." Do you recall the account that Senator Richard Neuberger gave, in an article in *Harpers,* of his discovery that he had cancer? "A change came over me which I believe is irreversible. Questions of prestige, of political success, of financial status, became all at once unimportant. In those first hours when I realized I had cancer, I never thought of my seat in the Senate, of my bank account, or of the destiny of the free world." He told that he had not had a quarrel with his wife since. "I used to scold her about squeezing the toothpaste from the top instead of the bottom, about not catering sufficiently to my fussy appetite, about making guest lists without consulting me, about spending too much on clothes. . . . I shudder," he said, "when I remember all the occasions that I spoiled for myself—even when I was in the best of health— by false pride, synthetic values and fancied slights."

As a matter of fact, our lives must be seen in the light of eternity if they are to make sense. Apart from this awareness of the wholeness of life, here and beyond death, events frequently are as puzzling as a paragraph isolated from the rest of a book.

The apostle knew how to face an uncertain future without fear because "whether we live or whether we die we are the Lord's" (Rom. 14:8). The Good Shepherd is unchanged, whether he ministers to our needs in the open field or in the fold. We do not voyage to some misty "beautiful isle of somewhere" but to a home "eternal in the heavens" that has been prepared for us by the Lord who set the seal of certainty upon his love "in that while we were yet sinners Christ died for us" (Rom. 5:8). The place and circumstances will indeed be new, but the love and fellowship will be familiar.

John Oxenham's comment is to the point, when he writes of a friend:

> *And death itself to her was but*
> *The wider opening of the door*
> *That has been opening more and more*
> *Through all her life and ne'er was shut.*
> *And ne'er shall be shut. . . .*

Isn't that precisely true? Death fully opens to the believer a door that has been opening wider with the years and through which the glory and grace of God have long been seen. It brings us into the fullness of that fellowship with God that has been ours since we first knew Jesus Christ. Have you noted that the church calls upon us to face the reality and the glory of death even in Baptism? There the pastor expresses the Christian hope that this babe, who has just received the Spirit of adoption, will be brought finally to "receive the fulness of [God's] promise in . . . [his] eternal kingdom." We are acknowledging that all of us must look forward hopefully to death, because we Christians know that then God will be able to give us far more than we have been capacious enough to receive in this present life, however long and full it may be. "For to me . . . to die is gain" (Phil. 1:21). That was true for Paul and for each of us. For death means that we share in the resurrection victory of our Lord.

This sounds like an Easter sermon, doesn't it? And it is, for we celebrate Easter fifty-two times each year. I have known church members to say, rather smugly, "Oh, I always come to church on Easter." If they did, they would be in their pew every Sunday. For we celebrate the Lord's resurrection every "first day of the week." We do so because we know that we share in its hope and power.

Our Lord's dramatic power over death was not first revealed to those who looked wonderingly into the empty tomb. As Dwight L. Moody once put it bluntly, "Jesus broke up every funeral he ever met." You recall the record of a little girl who had died. Her family sadly conformed to the mournful ritual of the day. In addition to the grieved faces of the bereaved parents and friends, there were the professional mourners, employed to add "body" to the lamentations that were to demonstrate the affection in which the deceased was held. Calmly but determinedly Jesus sent them out of the death chamber and closed the door behind them. Then, using the very words with which her parents had been accustomed to waken her every morning, Jesus said, "Talithe cumi! Come on, little one, it's time to get up." And she did.

There was another funeral, you may recall. The villagers of Nain were accompanying a widow to the graveyard to which she was taking the corpse of her only son. Again Jesus stopped the solemn proceedings to say, "Young man, get up." And another funeral was broken up because the corpse lived again!

It happened again at Jesus' own funeral, of course.

And ever since he has done it for every believer. Death loses its massive power. It is no longer the all-powerful monarch we have known it to be. Instead it has become a servant, fulfilling the Master's will in bringing us into the perfection of his fellowship.

The story is told of an old *abbé*, dictating a letter to a close friend from his deathbed. After a time he said to his secretary, "Write this: 'I am leaving the land of the living and will soon be with the dying.'" Then, as he thought over the words he had just spoken, he stopped her, "No, don't write that. That isn't true. Instead, write this: 'I am leaving the

land of the dying, and will soon be with the living.' "
One of our great contemporaries meant much the
same thing when he said to a friend, shortly before
the operation that was to result in his death, "Remember this: never will I have been so fully alive
as when you see me in a casket."

Simeon would have understood these men very
well, even though he stood on the other side of the
Lord's resurrection. He would have joined heartily
in the hymn that resulted from Henry Lyte's awareness of the fact that he suffered from incurable tuber-
culosis:

> *Abide with me, fast falls the eventide;*
> *The darkness deepens, Lord, with me abide.*
>
> .   .   .   .
>
> *I fear no foe, with thee at hand to bless;*
> *Ills have no weight, and tears no bitterness.*
> *Where is death's sting? Where, grave, thy victory?*
> *I triumph still, if thou abide with me!*
>
> SBH, 576

He does abide—with Henry Lyte, with Simeon, and
with us. "Lord, now lettest thou thy servant depart
in peace"—today, tomorrow, and through eternity.

"You stiff-necked people, uncircumcised in heart and ears, you always resist the Holy Spirit. As your fathers did, so do you. Which of the prophets did not your fathers persecute? And they killed those who announced beforehand the coming of the Righteous One, whom you have now betrayed and murdered, you who received the law as delivered by angels and did not keep it."

Now when they heard these things they were enraged, and they ground their teeth against him. But he, full of the Holy Spirit, gazed into heaven and saw the glory of God, and Jesus standing at the right hand of God; and he said, "Behold, I see the heavens opened, and the Son of man standing at the right hand of God." But they cried out with a loud voice and stopped their ears and rushed together upon him. Then they cast him out of the city and stoned him; and the witnesses laid down their garments at the feet of a young man named Saul. And as they were stoning Stephen, he prayed, "Lord Jesus, receive my spirit." And he knelt down and cried with a loud voice, "Lord, do not hold this sin against them." And when he had said this, he fell asleep.

Acts 7:51-60

Chapter VIII

The Martyr

(St. Stephen's Day, December 26)
Acts 6:8–7:2a, 51-60

It seems almost as if the ancient church foresaw our American temptation to sentimentalize Christmas. Of course, that is not the reason why the festival of our Lord's birth is surrounded by martyr days. The reason is rather to be found in the sober realization of the New Testament that "He came to his own home, and his own people received him not" (John 1:11). That tragedy of rejection is reflected also in the blood-colored paraments in the chancel on this day, as well as by the fact that round about this festival of joy the church has placed the days of commemoration for early martyrs. A halo of martyrdom envelops Christmas. For alongside this Day of St. Stephen there are the Days of the Holy Innocents and of St. John the Evangelist. There was profound wisdom manifested in these choices. The helpless babes of Bethlehem—who died because a cruel king ordered that innocent babes should die rather than have his throne threatened from even the most unlikely source—were martyrs in deed, even though not in intention. On the other hand, John was the only disciple to die a natural death, though, like his fellows, he was fully prepared to give this ultimate testimony to his faith. He was a martyr in intention, though not in deed. Stephen, of course, was a martyr in both intention and deed.

In time and mood his story is far removed from that of Christ's nativity. Yet they belong together. We should think of Stephen at Christmastime, for he is one who shows us clearly what it means to welcome the Christ.

I

Stephen speaks to us, first of all, concerning the obligation of true discipleship.

Celebrating Christmas is much more than reveling in sentimental "adoration" of the Babe. It is so terribly easy to permit the great fact of God's supreme gift to mankind to degenerate into the mushiness seen in the woman who protested that she couldn't find any Christmas carols that she could use at a party because they were all "so distressfully theological." Yet it may be that even she was nearer to the kingdom than those who wallow in an emotional ocean and are quite unaware of the Good News of redemption that the angels proclaimed and that our carols repeat.

Certainly Stephen rejoiced at the news that God

so loved the world that he had given this Christmas gift to men, but he knew that emotion is nothing if it is separated from life's totality. There was nothing very joyous about the situation that he faced. He was on trial, but his case was as rigged as that of any prisoner standing before a totalitarian court in our day. His judges had already determined upon his death. That was why he had been arrested. The formal proceedings were intended only to throw a mantle of legality over the lynching.

If you read Stephen's long address, it may well seem a bit dull and hard to finish. But it will not appear dull if you keep in mind the fact that this man was on trial for his life and that, instead of arguing his own innocence, he dares to accuse his judges of murder. That's both exciting for us and dangerous for him. But that is exactly what Stephen did. "As your fathers did, so do you. Which of the prophets did not your fathers persecute? And they killed those who announced beforehand the coming of the Righteous One, whom you have now betrayed and murdered, you who received the law as delivered by angels and did not keep it" (Acts 7:51-53). It is not too surprising that his judges were enraged and ground their teeth.

Witnesses to the truth of God have often had that experience. Ezekiel, for example, was warned that he was sent to a nation of rebels, impudent and stubborn. Nevertheless, he was to proclaim God's Word, that "whether they hear or refuse to hear . . .

they will know that there has been a prophet among them" (Ezek. 2:5). A modern preacher, standing in this line of apostolic succession, was once accused of "rubbing his hearers the wrong way." But his reply was, "That's not so. I'm rubbing them the right way; they ought to turn around." That is precisely what Stephen thought.

Stephen knew from the first that every believer must be a witness. No man commissioned Stephen to preach. He was selected as one of the seven men "of good repute, full of the Spirit and of wisdom" (Acts 6:3) to administer the distribution of charity in the Jerusalem church. But he knew very well that this did not exhaust his obligations as a follower of the Lord Jesus. So frequently and effectively did he speak to Jews in their synagogues concerning Jesus the Christ that they complained, "this man never ceases to speak" (6:13), and determined to silence him. They knew that nothing short of death could accomplish this. Like the shepherds of Bethlehem who "made known the saying which had been told them concerning this child" (Luke 2:17), Stephen was driven by an inner compulsion that was far stronger than any earthly appointment could be.

The fact that he was a "layman" had nothing to do with this fact. Important only was his status as a Christian. He would have understood the words of Sook Pong Snoi of Thailand, who told the International Missionary Conference at Willingen, Germany, in 1952, "Why all this theological talk about missions and witnessing? It is simple. You witness because you must. A new baby is born—it cries; a man is born in Christ—he witnesses. The more the baby cries, the more you know that it is a good healthy baby. The Christian is just like that." Another Asian, Bishop Azariah of Dornakal, has his Christian villagers put their hands on their heads (as if in the act of baptism) and repeat, "I am a baptized Christian. Woe is me if I preach not the Gospel." Stephen was such a man.

He knew, too, that witnessing with words is hypocrisy if our lives do not also witness to the same belief. His official assignment to distribute justly the food and clothing needed by the poor members of the Christian community was a part of this witness. "If a brother or sister is ill-clad and in lack of daily food, and one of you says to them, 'Go in peace, be warmed and filled,' without giving them the things needed for the body, what does it profit?" (James 2:15-16). Being a witness to the merciful love of God in his Son requires of Stephen that he do what he could to meet the physical needs of his contemporaries.

In our day the same obligation may be spelled out as "service to refugees," "inter-church aid" and the like, but it is the same obligation.

This work was put into proper perspective by one of our contemporaries, a biblical scholar who served on the committee of revision that produced the Revised Standard Version. His next assignment was with the Friends Service Committee, administering relief to the human flotsam of our stricken generation. Asked if he did not feel strange to move to an area of service so different, he replied, "But it isn't different at all. I've been translating the New Testament into new language for our generation; now I've the task of translating it to people in deeds of helpfulness. It's still the same work."

Even shocking and cruel death did not disturb Stephen's witness-bearing. As the crushing stones bore his body to the earth, he looked upward with quiet confidence and prayed, "Lord Jesus, receive my spirit." And, like the One who lived in him, he added, "Lord, do not hold this sin against them" (Acts 7: 59-60). Faith like Stephen's masters the fear of death, because it gives us assurance that the lordship of Christ is not limited to this temporal fraction of man's life. In the present hysteria that besets our world at the prospect of mass death coming upon us through the hydrogen and cobalt bombs, we who believe in Stephen's Lord have a magnificent opportunity to bear witness through the calmness and steadiness of our lives.

We have an equally relevant word to say to a divided world, a world of commingled hatred and fear of enemies. "Coexistence" between East and West is being violently rejected by many. But what other possibility is there except that of annihilation of one part by the other? That would be totalitarian warfare such as the world has never seen. And its outcome would be unpredictable. We destroyed the Kaiser once—to get Hitler; and Czar Nicholas, to get Stalin; and Tojo—to get Mao. Yet surrender would mean the cold terrors of the Nazi and Communist extermination camps. To condemn people to that would be evil also. Does our faith suggest any way out? Yes, there could be a creative transformation by which, as an ancient collect of the church puts it, "all our enemies may be led to true repentance, and may have the same love, and be of one accord, and of one mind and heart, with us and with thy whole Christian church." Be careful, however, before you buy that solution. It is not only our enemies who need to be transformed. We also need to be brought to true repentance, that the mind of Christ may be our master. But if this happens, and if we then sincerely pray for our enemies, who would dare to limit the possibilities?

But let us be clear about this. We do not bear this witness for the sake of any temporal gains that may come to us. We do not send missionaries to save ourselves or our world from Communism. We bear witness, in word and life, because we must. It is our Christian obligation.

II

The experience of Stephen would warn us of the cost of discipleship.

"His face was like the face of an angel" (6:15) and his words like those of his Master, yet the result was that "they cried out with a loud voice and stopped their ears and rushed together upon him. Then they cast him out of the city and stoned him" (7:57-58).

This aspect seems much more real to us today, even in comfortable America, than it did a few years ago. A few years ago persecution seemed to belong in the pages of the old books, but now it has become so common that it rarely hits the front pages of our newspapers. From one point of view we may rejoice that this is so. There is no insult so great as to be ignored. That has been the fate of the church for many years. It was treated with the disdainful respect one shows an elderly lady. The church was given a comfortable seat—and then ignored as far as the realities of life were concerned. Modern totalitarian states began the same way, but they learned that the church was astonishingly alive. Frankly, even the church was surprised at this revelation. That was when patronizing kindliness gave way to bitter hatred in these totalitarian states. This hatred is much healthier and much more complimentary. "The church of God is not a candle. Blow on!" These words of Edna St. Vincent Millay show the challenge that the church gives to those who oppose it.

Yet one would not dare to soft-pedal the tragedy that persecution brings to thousands. During the Japanese occupation of Korea, Christians were tortured to force them to worship at Shinto shrines. One believer was tightly laced in a wet leather jacket and then placed on a hot stone floor to dry out. When strangulation caused him to faint, he was brought back to the consciousness of pain by hypodermics. On the other side of the world, Nazis imprisoned and killed hundreds of Christians who refused to bow to Baal. In Communist-dominated countries like Latvia, a Red agent was stationed at the church door to note the names of those who attended church services. They were listed in the next group to be sent to a Siberian lumber camp. Anyone seen carrying a Christmas tree through the streets would probably observe the holiday in jail. In East Germany children who belong to the youth organization of the church have been barred from continuing their education. Hoodlum members of the Communist youth organization invade churches and attempt to disrupt their services. In Riga, 18,000 copies of a Lutheran hymnal found in a publishing house were all destroyed. In these and in hundreds of other ways, pressure is being brought upon the church today.

It is expensive to be a Christian. Yet there are many, who in other times were careless about their participation and loyalty, who have now discovered that the price demanded is cheap after all. "A mighty fortress" and "Lord, keep us steadfast in thy Word" have once more become the triumphant proclamation of a faith that does "not tremble at the brink of poverty or woe."

When Pastor Erich Schumann was arrested and

given a prison sentence, the Lutheran Church of Saxony issued a public statement to its members: "Whereas the sentence states that Pastor Schumann was responsible solely as an individual, we declare that he spoke as a servant of the church on the basis of the Word of God. Thus the sentence touches the whole church and those who preach the Word of God as their vocation. . . . We call upon the Christian community: Be untiring in intercession for our brother, Pastor Schumann. Be untiring in intercession for all who preach the Gospel. Be untiring in intercession for those in authority."

We are not members of the church triumphant but of the church militant, of the church "under a cross." In the midst of Christmas joy we must not be permitted to forget it. Our Lord said, "If the world hates you, know that it has hated me before it hated you. If you were of the world, the world would love its own; but because you are not of the world, but I chose you out of the world, therefore the world hates you" (John 15:18-19). Stephen, and many since him, learned how true these words are.

III

Yet who would feel sorry for Stephen or for any other martyr? We who have not tasted persecution dimly sense that they found the joyful reward of true discipleship.

I wonder where that sentence in the account of

Stephen's trial came from that says that the members of the court (his enemies) "saw that his face was like the face of an angel"! It could only have come from within that group. Might it not be that this was told to Luke by Paul? For Paul, then Saul the Pharisee, was one of those who sat in judgment and who actively concurred in the sentence of death. If that is its source, it would help us a bit to understand what happened later to this fiery Pharisee.

We do know that the memory of this judicial lynching stayed with him through the years, as a fire in his bones: "I am the least of the apostles, unfit to be called an apostle, because I persecuted the church of God" (1 Cor. 15:9). Was the memory of this look on the face of a dying man and of the forgiving words that answered the cruel stones at least a part of the "goad" against which Saul had been kicking (Acts 26:14)? We do know, certainly, that the torch of flaming witness that dropped from the hand of Stephen was picked up at last and carried to the very limits of the Roman world by "a young man named Saul" who "was consenting to his death" (7: 58, 8:1).

We may not forget that the Babe who lies so softly in the tender care of his mother is not helpless. Rather it is he of whom the prophet wrote: ". . . the government shall be upon his shoulder, and his name will be called, 'Wonderful Counselor, Mighty God, Everlasting Father, Prince of Peace.' Of the increase of his government and of peace there will be no end"

(Isa. 9:6-7). Much of the tragedy of our observance of his birth arises from our forgetfulness of this fact. He is the mighty Lord. The kingdom and the power and the glory are his, now and through eternity.

Neither is his church helpless before its enemies. In fact, the witness of the martyrs has been that only in the moment of persecution does the power of Jesus become unmistakably clear. So Bishop Ordass of the Hungarian Lutheran Church could tell the Communist judge, before whom he stood awaiting sentence, that never had he felt the joy and power of the Gospel to be as real as in the long months he had spent in a prison cell. Samuel Rutherford, imprisoned for the Gospel in Aberdeen, wrote a letter in which he gave his address as "the Palace of Jesus Christ" and said, "My Master doth give me great joy—good measure, pressed down, and running over." And John Bunyan, telling how he was taken from the courthouse to his cell on Bedford Bridge, wrote, "I did sing as though joy did make me sing."

One of the church fathers could say of his opponents in a period of fierce persecution, "Every man who witnesses this great endurance is struck with some misgiving. He is set on fire to look into it to find its cause. When he has learned the truth, at once he follows it himself." So many of our churches have failed to sound that note in our life and preaching. We seek to appeal to man's comfort and then wonder why the world passes by without interest. We try to compete with the entertainment facilities of the world, and come off second best. As Stanley Jones once put it, "They have swept out of the Protestant churches the crucifixes and put in cushions. Then they wonder why the cushions are not used." How strange that the church should be strongest when it is weak! But that is the central paradox of Christmas—a helpless Baby who is wholly dependent on the loving care of his parents is at the same time the King of kings and the Lord of lords.

How fortunate it is for us who belong to liturgical churches that we cannot approach our Lord's manger without also lingering at the tombs of the martyrs. Otherwise we might think that Christmas has no meaning for the dark tragic moments of life. We might conclude as did a friend of mine, "My wife died just before Christmas and since then that day has been meaningless to me." But Christmas is not tinsel, gifts, or even family joy. Christ was born into a brutal world, ruled by a dictator. Soon after his birth little children were slaughtered in cold blood in the hope of destroying a possible "pretender" to the throne. And his coming meant that many others would, like Stephen, have to give their lives for their faith.

Christmas is the day of celebration for the strong Son of God, immortal love, who will not be defeated.

Then Herod summoned the wise men secretly and ascertained from them what time the star appeared; and he sent them to Bethlehem, saying, "Go and search diligently for the child, and when you have found him bring me word, that I too may come and worship him." When they had heard the king they went their way; and lo, the star which they had seen in the East went before them, till it came to rest over the place where the child was. When they saw the star, they rejoiced exceedingly with great joy; and going into the house they saw the child with Mary his mother, and they fell down and worshiped him. Then, opening their treasures, they offered him gifts, gold and frankincense and myrrh. And being warned in a dream not to return to Herod, they departed to their own country by another way.

Matt. 2:7-12

Chapter IX

The Mysterious Strangers

Matthew 2:1-12

Little wonder that these dimly seen, yet majestic figures should have captured the imagination of mankind. The clouds of mystery that enshroud them only give them a firmer hold on our imagination. If you visit the magnificent cathedral in Cologne you may be shown the jeweled "Shrine of the Three Kings" and be given every detail you wish to know. You will learn that Gaspar of Tarsus was a bearded youth of 20, that Balthasar of Ethiopia was a black man of 40 and that Melchior of Arabia was about 60. Their remains are said to have been found by the relic-hunting mother of Constantine and later rediscovered by Cologne's Bishop Reinald in the twelfth century.

But the Scriptures are strangely reserved about them. We do not know the specific lands from which they came or the precise means by which they came to understand the message of the heavens. We do not even know how many Magi came to Judea. Early tradition, as reported by Chrysostom and Augustine, thought there were twelve, while others imagined that they numbered fifteen. Later their number shrank to three. The gifts that they brought to Jesus say nothing as to the number of the givers, since two men or a dozen might well have brought three kinds of gifts.

The title "Magi" suggests Persia as their place of origin, although commentators have noted that the ancient trade routes from Arabia entered Palestine "from the East" (the only clue the Bible gives as to their home). In ancient Medea there was a caste of Magi who performed priestly functions, and their descendants seem to have played a similar role in the Zoroastrian religion of Persia. Philo of Alexandria commended the Magi of his day for their research into the facts of nature, for their "true magic" and their sound reputation for character and learning. But in popular speech the name was applied to those who interpreted dreams and conjured up spirits. So again we find ourselves in a mysterious, uncertain realm.

One of the few details of which we may be certain, however, destroys the popular belief, fostered by carols, paintings, pageants, and even some sermons, that the wise men stood, together with the shepherds, at the manger on that first Christmas night. All the evidence of the Gospels is against this. Matthew's account of their visit pictures them as entering "the house" where "the child" was, while Luke has the shepherds finding Mary and Joseph, and "the babe lying in a manger" (2:16). The Magi found only "the child with Mary his mother," which suggests that Joseph, after having found a home for his family, was again working at his trade to support his wife and child.

Luke's subsequent story of the presentation of Jesus in the temple, an event that must have taken place at the end of the two-month period of ritual impurity of his mother, hints that this visit must also have preceded the visit of the wealthy Easterners. Mary and Joseph, who were devout Jews and profoundly thankful for the surpassing favor God had shown them, would scarcely have given the poor man's offering of two turtledoves if they had had in their possession the valuable presents brought by the wise men. In any event, it would have been far too dangerous to have gone to Jerusalem, Herod's own capital, after the death sentence of the child had been spoken. Then their only safety would lie in immediate flight to Egypt.

It is Herod who provides the final bit of evidence. To make certain the death of this "pretender to the throne," he ordered the murder of every child in Bethlehem "two years old or under, according to the time which he had ascertained of the wise men." Why such a wide margin of error if Jesus was still a newborn baby? But if several months or even a year had elapsed, this decision, though still terrible, would be understandable. Thus everything points to the fact that our Christmas artists have misled us. Of course, the traditional church year has sought to guard us against this confusion in that it separates the visit of the Magi from the day of our Lord's nativity and commemorates it on the Festival of the Epiphany.

But neither the Bible nor the church is too much concerned about the time sequence of these events. This and all the details of the visit are mere scaffolding. The real message of the Epiphany is much more important. What word do these mysterious and wise men from the East have for us, who like them would welcome Jesus at his coming?

I

Certainly their first word would be, "We must worship him."

How strange that the very mists that conceal the Magi enable us to see them so clearly. Or perhaps it would be better to say that the very fact that we cannot see their features enables us more easily to see our own in them. We ourselves are these men who followed a star in order that we might see magnified the glory and power of Jesus the Christ.

These sermons have called to our attention the people who, each in his own way, welcomed him at his coming. We have seen how the great words of ancient promise converge upon the manger at Bethlehem. But now we can also see that all the world's peoples meet at this same manger. The Good News of Jesus Christ is by its very nature a world Gospel.

It must of necessity include all mankind in its loving embrace. It must ignore the deepest differences that separate men—education, culture, wealth, nationality, and race. The Gospel of God's only-begotten Son is for all men, and these Magi, who came from the distant lands of the East to worship him, are symbols of the world-wide outreach of the Gospel. They are the first-fruits of the Gentiles, the first of a great stream that includes all of us who are non-Jewish Christians.

Though the historical basis of the Cologne legend is weak indeed, its theological truth is secure—in the Magi every race and continent came to the feet of Jesus, their Lord. The same truth is proclaimed by the traditional inclusion of a Negro in every creche. No wonder that our modern church should have designated the Epiphany season as that in which the world mission of Christendom is emphasized.

But this world-enfolding Gospel is not, in the first instance, a demand that calls negligent Christians to give more men and money for the evangelization of the whole world. Rather, it is the occasion for amazed gratitude that we, whom Paul correctly designates as "the uncircumcision . . . separated from Christ, alienated from the commonwealth of Israel, and strangers to the covenants of promise, having no hope and without God in the world . . ." have seen him who "came and preached to [us] who were far off . . . so then [we] are no longer strangers and sojourners, but [we] are fellow citizens with the saints and members of the household of God" (Eph. 2:11-12, 17, 19). We who are so blessed ought to sing our praises at this miracle of universal grace.

These wise men came to bow in adoration before him whom the church acknowledges to be Lord of lords and King of kings. They call upon us to do the same. Like them we ought to worship the Child because of what he is, because of the surpassing miracle of his birth. For greater than the strange star that led the Magi on their trackless journey is the event that the star commemorated: the fact that God has visited his people; that the day has dawned upon us from on high; that divine light has shined into the darkness of our sin. This mercy of God is the ultimate miracle. That grace is God's answer to man's futile revolt is the truly miraculous fact of Christmas.

How personal is the message that the mighty God cares for us! No wonder that Christmas and exclamation points go together. "O come, let us adore him!" So the Magi call to us across the centuries. We ought to heed their word. For if we know who it is that lies there in Bethlehem of Judea, we will surely come and worship him.

How inevitable it is that we gather as a congregation of believers even on a mid-winter day when snow and ice might well keep us within our homes. Yet many need the reminder spoken in 1622 to King James I by England's great preacher, Lancelot Andrewes:

"It was no summer progress. A cold coming they had of it at this time of the year, just the worst time to take a journey, and specially a long journey in. The ways deep, the weather sharp, the days short, the sun farthest off . . . the very dead of winter. . . .

"And we, what should we have done? . . . If rugged or uneven the way, if the weather ill-disposed, if any never so little danger, it is enough to stay us. Come such a journey at such a time? No; but fairly have put it off to the spring of the year, till the days longer, and the ways fairer, and the weather warmer, till better traveling to Christ. Our Epiphany would sure have fallen in Easterweek at the soonest. . . . To Christ we cannot travel, but weather and way and all must be fair. If not, no journey, but sit still and see farther. As indeed, all our religion is rather a contemplation, than a motion, or stirring to do aught." We dare not permit any obstacle to bar our way to Christ.

And all men must come with us, no matter where they live or what their race may be. This Christ whom we worship is a universal Christ. Even our American observance of his birthday reminds us of this fact, for we have borrowed from many countries and many centuries when we gather about a festively decorated Christmas tree to sing carols, exchange gifts, and wish one another happiness. It is as though every nation, every race, every culture, and every age has its gifts to lay as its token of adoration at the feet of Jesus of Bethlehem.

The wise men were wise indeed when they said, "Come, worship him."

II

Their second word is equally direct and simple: "We must serve him."

We cannot worship him truly unless our adoration finds expression in something more than words. There is essential truth in the Medieval inscription on the wall of St. Mary's Church in Lübeck:

God the Lord speaks to you—

> *You call me eternal—but you seek me not;*
> *You call me almighty—but you fear me not;*
> *You call me merciful—but you trust me not;*
> *You call me just—but you honor me not;*
> *You call me the Light—but you seek me not;*
> *You call me the Way—but you walk me not;*
> *You call me the Truth—but you believe me not;*
> *You call me the Life—but you desire me not;*
> *You call me lovely—but you love me not;*
> *You call me Master—but you serve me not;*
>   *If I condemn you, reprove me not.*

It is too often true. And is it not terrible that it should be true? How can there be such a hideous gap between the words that come so easily from our lips and the actions of our hands and feet? If we truly worship, then we must serve. Otherwise we hear the sorrowful, yet condemning voice, "Why do you call me 'Lord, Lord,' and not do what I tell you?" (Luke 6:46).

A major danger that confronts us as we engage in either public or private worship is that we use words that lack meaning because they are separated from the genuine devotion of our lives. Someone recently suggested that we ought to use this offertory prayer: "Dear Lord, in spite of all I say or do, *this* is what I think of you." Or in the words of another, "When you pray, 'Thy kingdom come,' your checkbook should say, 'Amen.'" If it doesn't, we had best force ourselves to answer the question whether we really mean what we have said. And since money is nothing more than a symbol of my time, ability, and labor, what is said concerning it must be said of the whole of my life.

It is proper, almost inevitable, that we should actively respond to the message of the Gospel. We should give to God, out of deepest thanksgiving, the very best we have, since he has given his best, "his only Son," for us. Little wonder that pious imagination has seen the shepherds presenting a lamb to the Babe and that the Gospel should record that these Magi should open their treasures to present him with gold, frankincense, and myrrh.

> *As they offered gifts most rare*
> *At that manger, rude and bare;*
> *So may we with humble joy,*
> *Pure and free from sin's alloy,*
> *All our costliest treasures bring,*
> *Christ, to thee, our heavenly King.*

SBH, 52

If our worship is genuine, we must serve him, obediently, sacrificially, and with dedication. The Magi give us the right example.

III

They are also right in saying to us, "We must proclaim him."

Evangelism in our own back yard and missions on the other side of the globe are not optional accessories. We are not free to take or leave them, as best suits our mood or convenience. If we are indeed Christians, we have laid upon us the inescapable obligation to proclaim him wherever our voice can be heard or our gifts carry the message.

Only the hardness of our hearts makes necessary a missionary command. The inner compulsion should be enough, for this news is literally "too good to keep." To withhold it from those who are still in darkness and under the shadow of death is not only a sin against our fellow human beings but a sin against the God whose love has reached out to them in such unutterable mercy and compassion. We must be evangelists and missionaries because we have a missionary God.

We need to be prepared to grasp every opportunity to "say a good word for Jesus" whenever there is a natural opening. There is nothing difficult or artificial about such witness-bearing. It is illustrated so forcibly in the Gospel record of the two young men who had just come to know Jesus but who could not keep quiet about him. Though it is perhaps harder to witness to one's own family, each sought out his brother with the simple word, "We have found the

Messiah . . . . Come and see" (John 1:41, 46). Even the Samaritan woman, burdened by a well-deserved evil reputation in her village, yet strengthened by a new faith, hastened back to ask the question, "Come, see a man who told me all that I ever did. Can this be the Christ?" (John 4:29).

Since there are those whom we cannot reach by our own voice, we can and must share through our gifts in making it possible for others to speak for us in Africa, Asia, and the other continents. There is but one mission, even as there is one world and one God.

We can be traitors to our Lord both by what we do say and by what we do not say. We are traitors if through our silence we fail to make known to others joyfully him who came to bring life and salvation to every man of every race. The wise men learned this as they stood adoringly before the Christ. Like Mary, they hid in their hearts all that they had seen and heard. How excitedly they must have conversed on their homeward journey!

Yet how little they really knew of Jesus. Unlike us, they knew nothing of the ultimate love of the cross and the matchless power of the resurrection. But since you and I do know so much more than they, our response in worship, service, and witness should be far greater.

The Author

Dr. John Schmidt is pastor of St. John Lutheran Church, Amherst, N.Y. He is a graduate of Wittenberg College and Hamma Divinity School, Springfield, Ohio, and Chicago Lutheran Theological Seminary. He also attended the University of Leipzig in Germany.

Before assuming his present position, Dr. Schmidt served parishes in Ohio, Michigan, and Virginia, and was director of the Lutheran World Federation Service to Refugees, Geneva, Switzerland. He also taught homiletics and biblical exposition at Lutheran Theological Southern Seminary, Columbia, S.C.

He is the author and translator of several books and a frequent contributor to national religious periodicals.